An Off-White Christmas

Advance Reader Copy

An Off-White Christmas

Donald G. Evans

Illustrated by Hannah Jennings

ECKHARTZ
PRESS

For the whole Flynn family, especially Terry—

this Christmas,
last Christmas,
next Christmas....

you're a part of us, always.

Acknowledgments

Many of these stories first appeared in literary publications: *Chicago Quarterly Review, Conclave: A Journal of Character, Xavier Review, Narrative Magazine, Pinyon Press, The Journal, StoryQuarterly,* and *Write City Magazine.* The title story was listed as one of the "100 Other Distinguished" in *Best American* the year it was published. Michael Jennings, my gifted copy editor, provided smart and meticulous editorial insight; his stewardship of this collection certainly made it better. Christine Sneed and Melissa Fraterrigo served as first readers for many of the stories. Stacy Foster helped a great deal with research for "Whatever's Left of Normal." I am enormously grateful to Hannah Jennings for her remarkable illustrations and design, which elevated this book from ordinary to special. My wife Margaret and son Dusty provided the inspiration and support needed to sustain the work.

Contents

An Off-White Christmas

I could hear Willie's moose-call "Maaaa" all the way upstairs. I stopped rummaging, stopped breathing. "Maaaaa." That was the year Pa died, and from my spot in the crawl space it wasn't too hard to believe in ghosts. "Maaaa." Toward the end, Pa had 100 pounds on Willie. He wore a beard where Willie hardly shaved. His hair was thin and white while Willie's was thick and black. "Maaaa." But close your eyes and you couldn't tell them apart.

The moose-call stopped, and I continued searching for my tree-buying outfit. Summer clothes, old drapes, Pa's pipe collection. Grade-school photos, Halloween decorations, Pa's army boots. Willie's mystery novels, Ma's cookbooks, Pa's famous people-biographies.

I lifted President Lincoln, and then General Lee. I sniffed Amelia Earhart. Old books gain weight and pick up a musty smell, just like old people. It made me sad, not just that Pa had died, but that a person leaves behind such bad clues.

By the time I got downstairs to the kitchen the spat was in full swing. "You ain't goin' shopping today, are you, Maaa? You have to have been born yesterday to shop today."

Day after Thanksgiving is Amateur's Day, to hagglers what the Super Bowl is to gamblers and New Year's Eve is to alcoholics. Ma says, "It's tradition, you go to experience the holiday season." Willie counters, "It's shopper's hell, you go to experience a tree up your ass." Ma always drags me or one of the other girls along to find our tree.

Ma wiped her hands on her rooster's apron and looked through Willie, as if he were an endlessly circling gnat. Ma opened the oven door, closed it. I had on my pink Nieman Marcus blouse and matching skirt I'd gotten the Christmas before. When Ma rose up, she patted the silk collar and said, "Now, Peggy, you go change out of that Zsa Zsa Gabor outfit."

Willie winked at me. I used to hate when Willie winked at me, but it was one of those things I got used to, and then it was one of those things I got to kind-of like, and then it was one of my favorite things. I held in a laugh.

My day-after-Thanksgiving outfit included mismatched snow clothes, broken boot buckles, popped buttons; Ma, of course, dolled herself down in Good Will clothes.

"I want to know who's falling for this beggar act, Ma," Willie asked.

Ma set the microwave for two minutes and hit start. She hrrmpped. "William Andrew, did you come all the way here just to be a royal a-hole?" When Ma gets in a huff, she uses variations of swear words: a-hole, h-e double toothpicks, son-of-a-beehive. Willie calls people pricks and jagoffs and cocksuckers.

To Ma, it's all a game. Willie's more sincere. He's been broke all his life, working jobs long enough to "get up a stake," and asking on the sly for me or one of the other kids to let him hold a ten until Friday. In every family, there's a rite of passage into adulthood: your first beer, moving to the adult table at holiday meals, the dropping of your nickname. In our family, you knew you were all grown up when Willie finally borrowed money off you.

Maybe that's why Willie always gets the best tree. Every Christmas since he's been on his own, Willie's beat Ma in the unofficial head-to-head competition. He instinctively knows value, and naturally thrives on negotiation. He sniffs out cheap, delightful gifts that everybody loves better than Ma's big-ticket presents. Willie, smug to his bones, boasts, "Nickel at a garage sale. Five cents!"

It's something to see Willie work. One time, Willie bartered down the price of a cheeseburger a buck. Another time, Willie low-balled The Gap on a sundress I wanted but couldn't afford. He's even gotten daily papers at less than the newsstand price. He looks at a sticker and declares, *That's not the price.* His theory, which he explains with hands pressed together in an inverted cone, is that *price* is the sector between what they'll sell for and what you'll pay. He points out flaws to managers, makes them take account of winnowing demand, and generally recasts items in altogether unattractive lights.

Me, I don't have the stomach for negotiations. In my opinion, you want to sell a car for two thousand, put two thousand on the window and let me decide from there. I hate that two thousand might mean a thousand, or it might mean fifteen hundred, or, hey, it might mean two thousand.

Willie and Ma bond over my incompetence. Willie still ribs me about the time I gave nineteen dollars for two ten-dollar pajama outfits on Maxwell Street. Ma declares, "You shoulda seen Peggy work." The truth is, I'd rather overpay than endure even a tiny amount of awkwardness.

The microwave buzzed, and Ma opened the door. Nothing in there. She closed it. I walked into the bathroom and changed. As I headed back to the kitchen, Ma straightened her patchwork tweed coat. She has a roly-poly shape, round face with short hair cropped to frame oval eyes, a biggish upper body and stumpy legs. "Lock up on your way out, Willie," Ma said. Willie, on the other hand, is one of those Jughead types who's never seen a chili cheese dog he didn't like, yet even in his late 30s keeps a telephone pole physique.

"They're going to beat you up again, Ma. I hate to see you get beat up again."

Ma stopped at the door, and turned toward Willie. "Worry about your own g-d Christmas tree."

"I will," Willie said. "In about three weeks."

A forest sprouted up from the icy blacktop parking lot on Laramie Avenue. Ma said we'd start there because she knew the man who ran it to be soft. "Cream puff," Ma said. "We'll steal the best one off his lot and get him to help us load it."

What I like about the day after Thanksgiving is the weather and the day off school. Work, now. It's crisp but not too cold, and shoppers flood the department stores and malls and dime stores. Many of the shoppers are in love. They split up, scour the city separately for just the right gifts, tingle with the thought of coming together again. They think this being in love is a good thing, but Ma could tell them otherwise. In her point of view, "Never fall in love. Once you're in love you'll pay too much." Love, according to Ma, is a seller's market; indifference a buyer's market. Willie's philosophy is simpler: "Screw them before they screw you."

There were eight or nine people at a tree lot the size of an index card. A seller's paradise, just like Willie warned. Ma stepped back to examine the first tree. She tsked, shook her head, moved on to the next. Here was this plump woman dressed in raggedy clothes, with a high wind swirling a tuft of snow around her scampy boots, examining trees as if they were paintings in the Art Institute. I stood beside her and waited to be of use. "I wish Julie was here," Ma said. "I don't know what's so g-d important she can't go tree shopping." Julie was in her grunge phase, and Ma, who the rest of the year sighed and said the neighbors must think we're on welfare, got goose bumps at the thought of turning tatters into holiday discounts.

As we got within earshot of the hunched-over man tending the lot, Ma said, louder than necessary, "I feel sorry for this one, Peggy. How's it ever going to find a home this Christmas?" It was one of the better trees on the lot: tall, full, green. The man blew breath into his bare money-changing hand. "Is good tree," he yelled. "Sturdy tree. Tall tree. *Good* tree." Ma didn't acknowledge the man, but said to me, "If Charlie Brown lived in the neighborhood, maybe. This is Charlie Brown's kind of tree."

Ma moved on to the next one. She tsked, moved on. Tsked, moved on. She circled back to the supposed Charlie Brown tree and lifted up the price tag. "Too much," she said.

All around us, parents and their kids picked out trees, paid the man, pulled their cars around to load. Ma held a branch and let it fall. The cold numbed my cheekbones. "Limp, already," Ma said. "This tree got cut down weeks ago." She studied it some more. She waved for the man to come over.

"I'm in a charitable mood and I'm thinking about taking in this orphan tree. What's the best you'll do on it?"

The man shrugged. "Forty, like it says."

Ma leered at the man, said, "Absurd" in a voice used to speak of mass murderers—Speck, Gacy, Dahmer. "Let's go," she said to me. "We're walking."

That's Ma's big line, "I'm walking," meant to throw a scare into the salesman, make him rush to her side and say, "God forbid, anything but that, please, ma'am, don't walk, no walking."

The man shrugged again. "Okay. You win. Thirty-five. Get it off my lot."

Ma's eyes glared out from behind a black ski mask with on-purpose holes in the eyes and mouth, and on-accident holes near the left ear. Ma said, "It's hard anymore to do a public good," this time in a voice reserved for assassins—Boothe, Chapman, Oswald.

We went to seven other tree lots. Customers outnumbered trees. As darkness came, even Ma must have been ready to admit the tree salesmen were sitting pretty. But then, we drove up to a little lot near Humboldt Park. The owner must have thought he'd pull people in from the park, but it wasn't working out. First off, his trees were all just okay. Second, it was all kids in the park, and kids don't have the money. Third, it was a neighborhood where even adults didn't have the money. Ma got a forty-dollar tree for twenty-five: a good deal, no doubt. But it lacked a certain something, that something that makes you stop and go: *wow, nice.*

I knew in my heart that come Christmas Eve Ma'd be faced, again, with a cheaper, better Willie tree.

When Willie walked in the house a week later, he said nothing about the height, or the fullness of the branches, or the beautiful blinking lights, or the golden angel on top. "How much?" he asked.

Ma rocked her chair. She tapped her fingers on the arm. "Twenty-five," she said. Willie stooped down and picked a handful of green pine needles off the white sheet covering the carpet. He dropped them. "Did they work you over out back first?"

Ma had had a couple spiked eggnogs, and she was in the mood to brag on herself. "Reminds me of how your father and I—mind you, this was when times were hard—how we chewed tree salesmen down to nothing. Noth-ing. Back then, it was absolutely necessary. We didn't have what you kids call *discretionary* income. Your father said it himself. He said, 'Rose, you could barter the socks off a shoe salesman.'" Maybe there was a time Ma bartered for her life, but not now. Now, she was a spoiled diva singing about oppression.

Willie walked around to the back of the tree. Ma kept on. "Your Uncle David, God rest his soul, could tell you how your grandfather insisted I negotiate the tree deal every Christmas. I had a knack."

"Why don't you hold a séance?" Willie said from behind the tree. "That way we could speak to all your witnesses."

Ma curled up her stumpy bare toes so they pointed to the ceiling. She lifted her eyebrows. "Go to h-e double toothpicks, William."

It had to be near-midnight just before Christmas Eve when Willie whispered my name and shook my shoulder. Pitch-dark separated me from Willie, but even blind and in a dream haze I could never mistake that voice. Either it was Pa come back to haunt me, or it was Willie. "Don't wake Maaaa. We're going tree shopping."

Maybe because Willie's the oldest and I'm the youngest, or maybe because Willie, despite all his faults, was the most dependable person I knew, for whatever reason I slipped on my coat and went with him. "No place is going to be open," I said.

"That's okay," Willie said.

No question, Willie was up to something on his no-good side. He roll-started the beat-up yellow station wagon he got in exchange for a snow blower he got for nothing. We crept down our block to the corner, neither of us speaking. As we passed the Mengarelli's he gunned it down a streetlight-brightened side street. "This prick car salesman sold me a dried-up one, Peggy. Pine needles fell off second day. Now, it looks like it's gone through chemotherapy."

"Win some you lose some, Willie. Buy another one tomorrow."

We were going fast, and Willie beeped once as he ran stop signs. Palmer Street was all parked cars and bare trees and dirty snow. I used my sleeve to make a tiny circle in the passenger's side window. Streaks of streetlight light ran across Blackhawk Park's ice skating pond. "I'd rather get a refund on this one," Willie said. "With interest for my time and troubles."

I pulled a hat and mittens from my coat pockets and bundled up. "Odd hour to be doing an exchange."

It hadn't snowed since early December, and all the old snow lay in heaps of hardened layers above the cement. You couldn't call it white anymore, more of an off-white. It looked like an off-white Christmas.

Willie slowed the car near Cicero Avenue, killed the headlights and turned into an alley. The car crept along, the crunching of ice and the whoosh of the heater blending with the busy Cicero Avenue traffic. We stopped. The fenced-in used car-turned-Christmas tree lot looked sleepy and content, the Cicero Avenue headlights acting as night-lights. "Are you sure there're no guard dogs, Willie?"

An unbroken string of unlit red, blue and green bulbs surrounded the fence like twine around a newspaper bundle. From the alley, I could see the back of a life-size plastic Santa. "Here's what we'll do," Willie said. "Give me a boost and I'll climb the fence. You wait behind the wheel. If anyone comes, drive off and I'll meet you in front of Ronnie's hot dog stand in fifteen minutes."

We got out of the car. I made a stirrup with my mittened hands, and Willie was over the fence. I slid behind the wheel. Willie went from

one tree to the next. He lifted branches, scratched the bark. Except for the breaking and entering part, it reminded me exactly of Ma's day-after-Thanksgiving tree shopping. Willie found one he liked and dragged it over to the fence. He gripped one hand around the trunk, and another around a branch, fought it until the tip rested on top of the fence. He hoisted from his legs, and flung it over. The tree rattled the fence as it somersaulted into the alley with a plop. I looked around, but nothing stirred. Willie went back to shopping. He finally found another one he liked, dragged it over to the fence and repeated. He did it one more time.

Then Willie climbed the fence and leaped down to the side of the tree pile. I got out of the car and helped him load the wagon—one, two, three. "This is stealing, Willie." I was losing my Christmas spirit fast.

"What he did to me was stealing."

"Maybe he didn't know. Did you try returning it?"

We were in the wagon now. Willie turned the key, and the engine chiggedy-chiggedy-chugged to life. Willie backed the car onto Palmer Street, and reversed direction toward Cicero Avenue. At the first break in traffic, Willie turned right and eased the wagon next to the curb. "What does that sign say, Peggy?"

A large piece of cardboard, fastened to the fence by coat-hanger wire, read: "ALL SALES FINAL—NOT RESPONSIBLE FOR DAMAGED MERCHANDISE."

"He knew," Willie said.

Willie dropped the car into drive, and as he did it sputtered and died. "Mother fucker," Willie said. He turned the key; it sputtered but wouldn't start. "I need gas, Peggy," he said.

Cold air blew out of the heater vents. The big plastic Santa hovered above us. A streetlight flickered bright then dim. Willie pulled his glove off with his teeth and reached into his pants pocket: about a dollar in change. I panicked. There in the beat-up old yellow station wagon, with three stolen Christmas trees in back, just outside the lot where they right-fully belonged, I thought sure we were going to jail. "Let's put them back, Willie. We can do it quick, before anybody knows."

"Calm down, Peggy. I need gas. The nearest open-late gas station's about a mile or so from here. I can cab down, pick up enough gas to get us back to Ma's, cab back."

The back window and the edges of the front window steamed. "Let me hold a five until Christmas Eve, Peggy."

I pictured my change purse sitting on my nightstand. Ever since we were kids, Ma preached to us never leave the house without carfare. That's what she calls it, be it for the bus or elevated train or a cab: carfare. "If something happens, at least then you got a way home."

"It's Christmas Eve now, Willie. Besides, I don't have any money on me."

Willie looked at the change in his bare hand. "I'll have to hitch."

The driver's door clicked open, and more cold air rushed into the wagon. Willie closed the door, and I rubbed up and down my arms to keep warm. Willie didn't put his thumb out so much as wave a stop-sign hand. Each car looked like a patrol car until it came close enough to see. Patrol car, patrol car, patrol car, late-model Sunbird. Patrol car, patrol car, patrol car, Aerostar minivan. Patrol car, patrol car, patrol car, delivery truck. My toes and fingertips hurt. Breath started to steam the side windows, and the back and front windows were freezing up. I rubbed a circle in Willie's window. Patrol car, patrol car, patrol car, yellow Checker Cab. It stopped. Willie opened the side door. I could see the back of Willie's head, and the face of a bearded Middle Eastern man. Willie looked back at me and waved, and the cab merged with traffic and was out of sight.

Steamy breath and below-zero air continued to do a number on the inside and outside windows. Soon, the whole car was frosted over, and I couldn't see a thing, only hear cars sounding like patrol cars as they whizzed past. It was like when I was a little kid, closing my eyes in full view, listening to Pa tease, "Where's Peggy? Did anybody see Peggy?," feeling invisible. I was in my own cold little world and what I couldn't see couldn't see me. I tapped my toes on the floorboard and clenched and unclenched my mittened fists to circulate blood.

In my head, I practiced my story to the cops. Sometimes I gave Willie up instantly in exchange for personal asylum; other times I clammed up and asked for an attorney, like all the guilty criminals on cop shows should do but don't. I debated with myself, would Willie know to come to the police station, or would he think I was kidnapped? Can they keep you locked up over the Christmas holidays? Was this an in-and-out type crime, or could you get a hard-ass judge and wind up doing life, like I'd heard about pot smokers?

A car engine slowed beside the wagon. A door clicked. Shoes rustled against pavement. For the first time, it occurred to me that this could be something worse than a cop—a robber—and I near fainted with fright until I heard a knock and Willie's Pa voice. "Pop the tailgate, Peg."

I reached over and pulled the black lever, and Willie lifted up the tailgate. He set down his milk-carton gas can. Next to him stood the cab driver, and the two yanked one of the three trees from the wagon. Willie reached his head inside. "Help with the gas."

I got out of the car. As I unscrewed the gas cap, I watched Willie and the cabbie carefully arrange the tree in the back seat of the taxi. Willie held up a finger, one second, and proceeded to root around the back of the wagon until he came up with a funnel. He slid it to me across the icy top. I poured the gas into the tank as Willie and the cabbie shook hands. The cabbie got back behind the wheel, and Willie slapped the back quarter-panel as the taxi, tree sticking out one window, left the side of the road.

When we were both inside the car, Willie started her up and I chucked the empty milk carton onto the back seat. "What was that all about?" I asked.

"Least I could do was tip the guy," Willie said. He rolled down his window and scraped ice off his sideview mirror. He reached with his right hand and adjusted the heater. "A few minutes it'll be nice and warm." Willie dropped it into drive and stuck his head out the window in order to see.

Our first stop, Willie delivered a tree to Snacktime Diner on the corner of Cicero and Fullerton. It was this all-night dive place where more people came to get out of the cold than actually eat. Willie'd been a regular there for years, and after he got back in the car he said, "Maybe that will help the Christmas spirit in that joint."

It was into the early morning hours, officially Christmas Eve. Soon enough, we'd all be gathered over at Willie's for pre-midnight mass dinner and the opening of some presents. The bigger celebration happened at Ma's house Christmas Day. The wagon was all toasty now, and I was sleepy. I looked back at the remaining tree and pictured it upright with dazzling, bright ornaments and magnificent lights and all the other homemade trimming touches Willie would somehow get done between now and dinner. I imagined Ma asking how much and Willie saying, "Nothing, Ma. I got it comp."

Willie turned off onto Lavergne Avenue, and killed the lights. He eased the car next to the curb. "What now, Willie?" He said, "One more stop."

He unloaded the last tree and hucked it over a short front-yard fence. It settled near the porch stoop of a modest little red brick bungalow. Willie quietly shut his door and halfway up the block turned the lights back on. "That was *your* tree, Willie."

"Nah. That tree's for Mick and Sandy. Mick's been on strike since summer and they couldn't afford one this year. Their kids shouldn't be without a tree."

"What about you? You don't have a tree, Willie."

"I got the chemotherapy tree."

When Willie dropped me off at the house, I snuck upstairs and got my change purse. I took out a ten for him to hold until after the holidays. "Don't tell Ma," Willie said. "She asks, we went out for a drink."

It was totally pathetic: balding, undersized, gold and silver tinsel hanging like snot from a kid's nose, lights that seemed to warn: CONSTRUCTION.

Ma stood frozen in the doorway, a shopping bag of wrapped presents in her arms and Willie, Jr. hugging her legs. Even from a distance and from an angle, there was no doubting the tree was a clunker. Willie's wife Jane took our coats, and Ma tried not to tip her hand when she asked Willie, "Where's the tree? I think I'll put the presents under the tree."

"I'll take the presents, Ma," Willie said. "You just relax. Don't bother about that tree." Willie winked at me. This was Willie's gift to Ma that first Christmas without Pa.

"No bother. My pleasure," Ma said. "This, I got to see."

Ma marched into the living room and stood before the tree, presents in hand. Between getting to bed late and getting up early, and with last-minute shopping and baking, memories of sitting frozen in the wagon on Cicero Avenue seemed remote. Lots of presents already rested under the sad tree. A low-budget string of lights wound through the branches. Each blink seemed like a dying effort. Some of the family was already there, some on their way, all of us silently dealing with the fact No Pa, and wondering who'd pass out presents. Ma scattered our presents underneath the tree, and as she stood grabbed a handful of tinsel and asked, "How much?"

"Twenty-five," Willie said. "On the lot it looked like a great tree, but right away the needles fell off." Ma's roly face turned cherry-pie red, and she pursed her lips to hide a smile. "It looks better with the lights off. Turn off the light, Jane." The room went dark.

"No refunds?"

"No refunds."

A last-gasp twinge of light provided a brief look at Ma and Jane and Willie, Jr., and that poor Christmas tree, and then everything went dark again. From my angle off to the side, Ma looked bigger than the tree. "You got beat up, William." Another twinge of light.

"I got beat up, Maaa." Darkness again.

Ma picked up Willie, Jr., who squiggled loose, and the doorbell rang again, more gift-bearing relatives, and I felt happy and content. Ma was wrong, I knew that then. Love had its price, but it was never too high. Willie, Jr. ran to the door, and Ma and Jane followed. I listened to the garbled high-pitched exchanges as the lights made it through one more blink. I caught a peek at all the packages under the tree, and then pictured them in my head like a memory game.

I stole a look at Willie, who was stooped down reading tags. I couldn't tell, in that moment, whether Willie winked at me, or whether the blinking lights had made it seem that way. It went dark again. I waited for the light to fight back on, waited for Willie to pass out the first present.

Every Day's a No Repeat Day

A blaring, flashing paramedic wagon backed into the old couple's drive-way somewhere just that side and way this side of sitting-on-the-porch weather. I pulled back my curtains. It was dark and the window was fogged and my contacts were blurred, but I could see that somebody got carted out of there. I plopped down my stairs two at a time. I stood just inside the cracked front door while flashers flashed. An eye, a cocked half-face; a soft cloud of breath, folded arms; a chin to a cell phone, a nose to glass. Scenes changed, shoop-shoop, like a ViewMaster, and then the wagon sped off, siren wailing, and eyes and half-faces and chins and noses retreated.

I heard his voice: *She's getting temperamental.*

I heard her voice: *I don't know why we didn't get rid of that thing years ago.*

This old couple was about as old as old couples get. A write-up in the local newspaper said they had just celebrated their 75th wedding anniversary. Seventy-five *years*: I'd have to hit the streets running to even contend for that. Say I found a woman I loved, got her to love me back, and we eloped to a drive-through Vegas chapel—we'd still have to both make it into our low hundreds.

I never knew their names until the article. Alphonse and Marjorie Ori. The article said Al retired from the Syracuse police force 35 years prior, which was a fair sight longer than I'd lived. Marjorie ran the house and raised a bunch of kids, how many I don't remember, a whole bunch.

I thought sure one or the other was dead.

The *da Da da Da, da Da da Da, da Da da Da, da Da da Da* woke me from a blank, drowsy bout with my studies. I opened one eye and peered out my window, as if through a keyhole. Ancient sugar maple and oak treetops arched over the head of Jasper Street, in front of St. Andrew's Catholic Church. It was there that two narrow bands of rollicking asphalt joined, then, continuing as one concrete crusader, divided Jasper Street in half, dead-ending at the Oak Street tee. The shriveled tan and orange and auburn leaves formed a western canopy to our block.

By the time the last of the six resounding bass dongs sounded—DOOOOONGGGgggg—I was out the door. That was the moment when the side of Jasper Street with all the cars became illegal, and the side with no cars became legal. Six o'clock every night. The alternate parking law, designed to facilitate sweeping and especially snow removal, permitted parking on just one side of the street at any given time. Even and odd, going by street addresses. Every night, back-to-back odd days not included, I moved my car.

The old man's DeSoto had accumulated three parking tickets, and I now considered what could or should be done to prevent more. Alphonse had not really driven since the Nixon era, but tottered out daily to start and move his car. It took the rest of us a few minutes, him half an hour. Once a month or so, he unsteadily topped off the tank with a plastic funnel and big metal gas can I assumed somebody else filled for him. Not now; not since the ambulance.

Al bought his hulking sedan new—*brand* new—in 1942. It still only had 100,000 original miles on it. Al had walked a beat around the university district and Marge never learned to drive, so minus a couple family vacations, they'd put only a few miles here and there on the old classic, and then after he retired it became mostly a fond memory of life from those heady post-war days through the birth of rock-n-roll on into Woodstock, the Civil Rights movement, Korea, Vietnam, disco, the computer era, the MTV revolution, corporate boom and bust, one Iraq war then another. *She just doesn't have any getup and go left in her.*

I'd pieced together the car's history in much the way I'd pieced together the biographies of my other neighbors—snatches of 30-second conversations, as we moved cars.

I thumbed the parking tickets as darkness rapidly descended. The insurance salesman with the '88 metallic brown Skyhawk said he got a definite i.d. "It was the old guy," he said. "I could see it from my window. No doubt about it." He started his car and exhaust burst out the hole in his muffler. The blonde nurse wiped raindrops off her '96 ice blue Dodge Avenger's windshield. Sometimes, I thought she was the one. "His hand moved," she said. "He was moving when they loaded him into the wagon." She chugged off.

The hard wrrr of engines punctuated the echoing dooooong. I thought about our delicate connection to one another, of how our eyes, at the moment when the ambulance rushed down Jasper Street, were fixed on a single blip in the universe.

The out-of-work carpenter waved. His light cashmere Volare station wagon with woodtone trim wore several coats of etched-in dust. The carpenter continued a conversation from the night before, or maybe it was the night before that. "According to Farmer's Almanac, this is just the beginning. It's going to be a bad winter. The Farmer's Almanac's always dead on."

"You should be just about finishing up here, shouldn't you?" asked the cute bank teller with the owlish face and streaks of absurdly premature gray hair.

Sometimes, I thought she was the one. The truth was, they all seemed, at one time or another, like the one. But I was shy. I never imagined what I wanted from a woman, but wondered, rather, what she could possibly want from me. I suppose if any one of them had said, "What are we waiting for?; let's go," I would have been off. But they didn't. "Yes, hopefully," I said. The driver's door of her Dreamsicle-colored Love Bug clicked open—"Good for you," she said—and then slapped shut.

I'd already taken four and a half years to complete a four-year political science program, and now just Economics 102—a general requirement—stood between me and graduation. It was my only class that fall. Economics 101 had baffled me, and I'd put off and put off the follow-up course. Here it was, the first of November, and it seemed certain to hold me hostage in Syracuse, New York. Despite all my studying, reading and extra tutelage, the information seemed like chatter going off in my still head. It should have been a time of giving landlords notice, booking U-Hauls, planning the future. But it would have been like dressing for a party to which I hadn't yet been invited.

"Probably one of them didn't take their pills," the too-much-makeup corporate trainer with the gold Trans Am said. "You get to their age, you gotta remember to take your pills or that's it." Sometimes, I thought she was the one, and I thought that now as her window squeaked up, up, up until it sealed her into her car.

"Could be a problem with breathing," the short order cook with the green Gremlin said. "They get breathing problems, they got to go in to get straightened out."

We were shouting at each other from the length of a car, or two, or three. Keys in hand, shoulders twisted toward our driver's doors, we were poised for the shortest of conversations.

I left the tickets under the DeSoto's wipers, and started my own car. I loved that sound. I made that car from a shell—rebuilt 289-2v-8-cylinder, rebuilt c-4 tranny, reproduced fiberglass trunk lid and chrome bezel, parts from a dozen cracked-up '68 Mustangs, '68 Shelby convertibles and '65 T-Birds. Besides the investment I'd made in a college education it was all I had.

Here was the other thing: I didn't want to be whatever it is you became when you got a political science degree. I'd spent going-on five precious years of my life and all my savings, only to discover I wanted to be what I'd already been. I was a middle kid from a big Greek family. A college education had always been my parents' colossal dream for me—*do you want to lie in a puddle of oil all your life, Cojo?*—and that pressure, along with my own desire to be something more than a grease monkey, led me here. I'd enrolled at 24, old for an undergraduate: so old most of my peers looked at me as a guy that could buy them beer. Now, it would be embarrassing, a failure, to revert back to being a mechanic, worse, by far, than the second worse thing I could imagine, and yet that was what, in my heart, I wanted to do. I loved being in our garage on a Saturday afternoon. We lived almost at the junction of two major highways in a neighborhood of Blacksburg, Virginia, known as Stroubles Mill. There in that oil-scented little Utopia—engulfed by the hum of high-speed engines, sun streaks coming in through the open overhead door, the Hokies on the radio, neighbors stopping to chat—days passed like minutes.

I loved following a rattle-rattle or chink-chink through to the next clue, developing a theory and then testing it. I loved trips back and forth to the auto parts store and the junkyard. I loved the junkyard: pile after pile of precious metal parts.

The oldies station shook my speakers. I turned the volume down a notch. I looked out over my shiny blue hood. This central New York weather was slowly eating away at my '68 California Special Mustang's mint condition, but I couldn't afford to garage it. I drove the length of the block and turned around in the church lot. *Johnny B. Goode* ended, and the disc jockey said, "Every day's a no repeat day." In the time it took me to start my car, drive to the church lot or the Oak Street tee, depending on even or odd, I might get through half a song. *Heartbreak Hotel. Run Around Sue. My Boyfriend's Back. The Twist.* I parked.

She stood there, assessing the parking tickets, and watching the moving cars like a game of follow-the-leader. I looked at her, she looked back, and I knew for certain she was the one. "I'm his granddaughter," she said. Behind the wheel of the old guy's enormous steering wheel, she looked tiny and slightly afraid, and when the engine bellowed to attention her hand let go the key. I walked over to the car and motioned for her to roll down the window. "Keep your foot on the gas, just a little…let it rev thirty seconds or a minute before you put it into drive."

Heap of junk, is what it is.

Not worth the aggravation anymore.

The granddaughter managed, but barely. When she cut the engine, her face continued to vibrate, or so it seemed. She looked relieved to be done with a fierce wrangle and determined not to engage in another. I gave her a little wave, intending to return to my apartment, when she hurried over. "You know my grandma and grandpa?" she asked.

I nodded. "How are they?"

She shrugged, as if to say, "Not good," "It's hard to tell," and "Time's just about up," all at once. She continued, "I'm only here a week—I wanted to get out here and see them, you know? But Grandpa, he doesn't need to be doing this anymore. I have to run it by him…what's your name?"

"Cojo."

She said her name and I almost simultaneously forgot it. "Would you be willing to move this car for him? I mean, you move your own anyway, right?"

The '42 DeSoto featured, for the first time in any car, pop-up headlights that Chrysler called "Air-Foil Lights." Its motto was, "Out of sight, except at night." I glanced now at the car's dinged-up waterfall grill and its soiled whitewall trim rings. I tried not to gawk. "It would be no trouble," I said, trying to disguise the sudden, inexplicable arousal that'd come over me.

The bell tower chimes went off every hour on the hour, but I hardly noticed them except at six p.m. The melody, which stayed in my head long after Jasper Street had grown silent, sounded familiar, but the lyrics eluded me—*da Da da Da, da Da da Da, da Da da Da, da Da da Da.*

During the soft *da Da da Da* das men buttoned shirts and fumbled through work pants, women slipped into shoes and rooted through

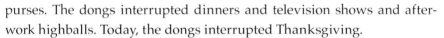

purses. The dongs interrupted dinners and television shows and after-work highballs. Today, the dongs interrupted Thanksgiving.

The season's first snow fell.

The ambulance had come and gone four times total. The granddaughter told us Al had been in and out. The second time, everybody had it figured for a relapse. But that time it was Marge. The third time Al again. It was a teeter-totter of potentially fatal illnesses: up, down, Marge, Al, heart attack, stroke.

Now, though I couldn't see the old couple from my window, I knew they were both home.

My own Thanksgiving was a potpie and work on an extra credit paper. My mom and dad were disappointed I couldn't make it home for Thanksgiving but were consoled by the thought of me coming home, maybe for good, around Christmas. Would there be a big ceremony for them to attend? Had I found a nice job somewhere near home? Had I thought about the fact that I was going to need a few new suits and other clothes? What kind of salary could somebody with a political science degree expect?

I thought about the crowd of cousins and in-laws and assorted friends gathered at my Uncle Ted and Aunt Vasso's house. We were a family with deep roots in a college town but no college graduates to our credit. My parents thought of a college degree as something akin to gold, something that could be cashed in for actual money. I'd become a kind of family celebrity because of college, and from here I didn't think I could drop back to the way it was before. I felt great shame in advance of my failure.

I took the granddaughter's keychain from my pocket. I looked guiltily across to the old couple's porch.

It had so far been a mild winter, but anybody who'd lived in Syracuse knew to take that for what it was worth. Once it started snowing, it hardly ever stopped, and at some point the whole town would become a gigantic slush ball.

I had this sense that if Al and Marge could just make it through to a new sitting-on-the-porch season everything would be perfect. I had the same sense about myself. I concentrated on Al and Marge's window. I popped the hood. *Just get through this rough patch*, I told myself. *Get to the other side.*

The linguistics professor scraped the ice off his Chrysler Cordoba's back windshield, and I brushed the snow off my Mustang's Presidential blue hood, and the nurse kicked her tire. The bells donged. "You ask me, it's lights out," the linguistics professor yelled.

Everybody had cars. Outside the university Syracuse was strictly a driving town. Upstairs, in my one-bedroom apartment, I kept a 64:1 die cast car collection, an extension of a larger collection back in Blacksburg. Every time a new car arrived on the block, I tracked down the Matchbox or Hot Wheels or Johnny Lightning equivalent and added it to my collection. I had the VW Beetle and the Trans Am, I had the Skyhawk—wrong color and year, but close. I had the Volare station wagon and the Gremlin, the '42 DeSoto, of course. I parked those miniature cars along my living room shelves—I had it organized, like Jasper Street, into two sides—and read up on them in library books.

I'd gotten a crack at several of them, partly because fixing a woman's car was, for me, flirting. "Let me take a look," was my big pickup line. I'd tricked out the Cougar's exhaust and replaced the squealing water pump; adjusted the Honda's idle and replaced the timing belt; patched the Jaguar's body with a little bondo and paint. I should have been getting money for this—I'd been *offered* money—but I guess I loved gratitude so much more. Plus, I didn't know if I was using the cars to get to the women, or the other way around.

"I hate to say it but you only get so many strikes," the nurse said.

Though I didn't see their names in the obits, I sometimes thought the same thing: one or the other was dead. The ambulance, now a regular event, had come again the previous night. Again, we'd left our apartments and watched the ambulance load up and leave. A blanket had covered Al's whole body, including the head, and Marge was helped in beside him. I'd gone out there in just a sweatshirt and slippers. The steam from my breath had cut through delicately falling snowflakes. Ice covered all the bare tree branches so that from a distance, through shards of streetlight light, it appeared silvery and festive, especially with snow sticking to fat branches.

I hadn't meant to rebuild the car, but in just a short time I'd begun to care for it like my own. At first it was just a few minor adjustments—replacing the heavy-duty starter button, cleaning out the old distributor cap, installing a new crankcase pan magnetic bolt, changing the stainless steel wiper arms and blades—that I got done in the early morning before I headed to class and before Al and Marge might be awake. Then—I couldn't help it—I bought a set of old stock shock absorbers, including bushings, out of my meager savings, and once I did that it seemed a shame not to replace the upper support pins. Then it was the brake linings and the head gaskets. I found myself investing in hard-to-find parts, like the cigarette holder built into the steering wheel.

I leaned now on the DeSoto, long after my neighbors had retreated to the warmth of apartments and houses I didn't know, wouldn't know, from the inside. My ears and toes grew numb. It was such an intricate, complicated machine, and so much could be done to make it better. To make it right.

The electrician with the revoked license who moved his girlfriend's apple red Sunbird nights she slept over said he knew somebody who knew the old couple. "They refuse to stay in the hospital, is what it is," he said.

I walked over to my Mustang and started her up. It was persistently but not yet miserably cold. That was coming. The whole operation of moving cars from one side of the street to the other became much more tedious. There were windows to scrape, engines to warm, sometimes tires to inflate.

I sat behind the Mustang's deluxe steering wheel and listened to *Double Shot of My Baby's Love*. The windows fogged from the inside. When the song ended, I got out of my car. I stood between the DeSoto and the Mustang, allowing ample warming-up time. The corporate trainer snuck up on me. "Hi there," she said. Nobody knew anybody's name, though I'm sure at one time or another we'd all introduced ourselves. That first time, we were hardly listening, or we forgot, and then forever after it felt foolish to try again.

"Any news on the old guy," she asked.

"Nothing that I know of," I said. "I hope he's okay."

"It's just so hard on the family. I went through a terrible time when my dad died." Then, "I saw you working on their car."

I nodded, not giving anything away. She started her Trans Am and I cringed as she immediately dropped it into drive. The policeman we called Officer Fatso cruised down our block at six fifteen sharp every day, and it was getting to Officer Fatso time. I put the DeSoto in gear, turned up the radio. It was an original Model CR-76 radio that received AM only, and I thought of it as living history. I listened to *Blueberry Hill* as I drove up the block, into the church parking lot, and back to the other side of Jasper Street. After I'd parked, I tuned the radio back to the station it had been on when I'd first moved it. I wondered if this was necessarily a good goal, to return things to exactly the way they'd been before you got there.

The phone startled me from a deep nap, and I lunged for the receiver. A husky, ancient voice said, "Your car. He's out there." It took me a second to get my bearings. "You get to him now he might tear the ticket up." His voice strained to make it to the end of the sentence. The phone clicked. Without thinking, I scooped up my keys from the table, slid my feet into shoes, and bounded down the stairs. Officer Fatso ripped the ticket from his pad and stuck it under my wiper blades.

I noticed right away that the DeSoto had already been moved, and wondered how Al did it at his age and whether he heard any difference in how the car ran.

"Can't you give me a break?" I asked.

"It's six-thirty," he said. "Six-fifteen is a break."

He got in his car and drove off toward the Oak Street tee, and then turned up the hill toward campus. Officer Fatso must have had a pretty clean plate in order to stick to his drive-down-our-block schedule. Maybe in the past neighbors had made complaints, or maybe Officer Fatso had a grudge against somebody on the block. The only other ticket I got was my first night in Syracuse. Perched on the flat roof outside my second-floor apartment window, I had felt, at once, free and lonely. I knew not a soul, but then again: I knew not a soul. I'd gotten a birds-eye view of Officer Fatso, then just this fat cop, ticketing my car. I'd gone down to check the ticket. I'd looked across the street. Cars had lined the curb up to Oak Street and far down the keyhole. I'd checked my side. Just my Mustang. The ancient man had pointed a finger. "Odd day," he'd said. The ancient woman at his side had said, "You got to move your car. Six o'clock every night, you got to put it on the other side."

Now, my car again stood alone on the even side of Jasper. I looked at the old man's face pressed against his window. I waved. He shook his head, as if to say, "That's a shame," and then gave me a two-finger salute. No sign, from where I stood, that Al had sniffed out his impending surprise party. I recalled giving Alphonse my number on that first day. He apparently collected them for just this purpose—in anticipation of doing his neighbors a good turn. How many thousands of times, over the years, must he have scanned the street?

I started my Mustang and slowly, carefully began scraping all the windows. No hurry now. Winter—I mean *real* winter—had set in, and my savings had run out, and my loan money had run out, and I had become uncertain whether passing that bastard class was what I truly wanted. It had been gray for days and weeks on end. I wondered how often, if ever, the old couple's kindness was returned.

When I looked back at the old couple's window, they both stood there, their faces pressed to the glass, and though their images were obscured by the bad weather I was sure I saw Al leaning on Marge and Marge leaning on Al. In my head, their troubles had been going on forever, but as I thought back they'd been sprightly and cheerful—no sign of any bad to come—just three months before.

It dawned on me, as I pulled a u-ee at the Oak Street tee to the beat of another no-repeat day, that the impending tragedy was not that one of them would soon be dead. It was that the other would still be alive.

I used to like even days better because I lived at 218, and I liked to see the Mustang so close to my front door. But there was that one odd day every once in a while, the 1st after the 31st, when you didn't need to move your car at all, and that used to be my very favorite day. But now I dreaded an odd-odd sequence because I didn't want to miss another minute of my few minutes left on Jasper Street.

A spark was missing. I'd ordered what I needed from the auto parts store, and worked under an inspection lamp in the cold. While I was at it, I did a complete tune-up. Just a few more tweaks and adjustments, along with a new starter, and she'd feel young again. I waved to Al, but concealed my present to him. Christmas Day, I'd get him to sit behind the wheel and listen to that purr. Wouldn't that, at least for a few fleeting seconds, return him to his younger days and show him that life was, or could be, a continuum and not a downward spiral?

Soon, my Mustang and I would ride into Blacksburg—we were known as a set, like an old married couple—probably never to return to Syracuse. I wanted to know, somehow, that I'd left things a little better.

The term ended a week-and-a-half before Christmas and all the students except me headed away from Syracuse to someplace else for the holidays. My professor gave me an incomplete until he could review all my extra credit work, which would be after the holidays. My test scores were the scores of somebody who'd wandered off the street into the wrong class-room, but I might sneak through on earnestness and effort. I'd decided to stick it out until something went right or everything, officially, had gone wrong. I'd already called home to wish everybody a Merry Christmas, and one-by-one my family had taken the phone to do the same.

I thought of what my life might become. Through the window, I studied the snow splattering against cars and houses, the wind spritz-ing powder over recently shoveled walks, a woman tumbling, fruit cake dropping.

It surprised me more than a little when the Da DA, Da DAs started. Darkness had fallen. Instinctively, I buttoned my shirt, put on shoes and a coat.

It was a ballet of cars and people: a gauzy, sideways snow fell, church chimes rang, ignitions pierced the silence like so many blown kisses. Everything was white. The corporate trainer's gold Trans Am staggered up the block. The aerobics instructor's puffy pink jacket orbited her Cougar. The nurse's pointy red wool cap disappeared inside her Avenger. The Skyhawk's tailpipe billowed gray smoke.

I clutched the DeSoto's keys in my bare right hand. I'd had no permission to fiddle with the old couple's car. I should have gotten permission. But didn't the essence of this gift demand surprise? As a mechanic, you see the bruises, hear the gasping, feel the age. Your hands get dirty. Al would get to experience the car fully restored, which meant he would be transported back to a shiny, innocent time before the deterioration.

Then the ambulance turned the corner. The cherry top was dull and silent as tires crunched pavement and glided to a stop in the driveway.

I never saw snow like I saw those years in Syracuse. A surreal stream of perpetual white flakes filled the air, almost like an illusion. Snow settled on my coat, my hair, the tops of my shoes. The St. Andrew's chimes completed their sequence but now, in the place of all those Das, I heard, *through the age-es, peace and good cheer.*

The ambulance driver shambled past me with a nod of his head. One of them had finally died. "Hey," I called after him. He looked back. "The old guy," he said. I turned to look at the DeSoto; a smidge of black paint poked through all that white. There would be no final joy ride to remind Al of his youth, and whatever days remained for Marge would be painful and barren.

Neighbors gathered. A fierce wind whapped the street, but none of us felt it, hardly, through our layers of winter protection.

You Have to Go to the Snow

Barf break!

Puke stop!

Pulling over!

The U-Haul's taillights blinked ten yards ahead. I adjusted the Oldsmobile Alero's rearview mirror while Mom, in the passenger's seat, and my teenaged son Georgy, in the back seat, settled in for the 1,500-mile drive. Janine and Paulo's Chevy Cargo Van crept behind us. There were seven vehicles in all. A lightning-bolt ffffffft penetrated the 4 a.m. silence. "Midge?" Papa's tentative voice asked. "Midge? You there?"

"Shush," Mom said. "Your papa's talking." She turned her walkie-talkie toward her face. She carefully, deliberately pressed the button. She yelled, "OKAY, YEAH."

We followed Papa onto Lakeview Avenue. We stopped at a red light: the U-Haul, the Alero, the Cargo Van, the Dodge Durango, the Isuzu Rodeo, the blue Mitsubishi Eclipse, and finally the light blue Mitsubishi Eclipse. We sat bumper to bumper to bumper to bumper to bumper to bumper to bumper. "Mom," I said, "Release the button."

"...two, three. MIDGE!!! You have to let go the button," Papa screamed. "Testing, one, two, testing."

We followed Papa up the pitch-black entrance ramp and merged onto the pitch-black highway. Roadside reflectors and our headlights gave shape to the landscape. We plunged ahead. As I fluffed my hair in the rearview mirror, I watched Georgy flex his triceps. West Palm Beach, Florida, began to dim and Baraboo, Wisconsin, brightened. "IT WORKS," Mom yelled.

Papa had lost his job—*forced retirement*, they called it. In 65 years, or at least since his first paper route, he'd never been out of work. They'd sold the house, liquidated assets, and recruited the whole family to move them back north, where rent was cheap and Papa could immediately find part-time work.

"This way, too, we'll be there for Grandma Winsconsin," Mom had said. Grandma Winsconsin didn't have many Christmases still in her. She lived in an old people's home near relations on Papa's side. We often threatened to visit, but the time never seemed perfect to see a senile relative on the other side of the country.

In a private phone consultation, Petey said we had to do this. Jack said Papa wouldn't ask if it weren't important. Janine said, "Okay, but does it have to be Christmas?"

Papa had said, "You have to be gone on the closing date or else you get hit with huge fines. They could throw you out on the curb, it's within their rights."

Papa's voice had betrayed the tiniest trace of desperation, despair, or something like panic. He needed our help. We generally took vacation to accommodate Christmas in West Palm Beach, and miraculously we were all able to extend the time for this cross-country journey. Some of us lived locally but others had to drive fair distances just to get to the starting point. Georgy and I had flown. Mom said it would be like when we were kids, driving north toward Grandma Winsconsin's and the snow.

That was how we always pronounced it, long after we knew better: *Win*-sconsin, as if the prize were a 'sconsin.' Papa had moved to Florida when he was just a teenager, to manage a gas station his dead father's old war crony had bought. The gas station didn't last but West Palm Beach did.

For Christmases during my childhood, when the winter sun warmed the green, lush landscape of our adopted Southeastern home, we made off in one station wagon or another toward the frozen, white tundra of Papa's native Midwestern home. Because of Papa's vacation schedule, we every year raced to make it to Grandma Winsconsin's in time for Christmas dinner. The way was strewn with fog and black ice and blinding sunshine and floods and road closings. It was an obstacle course of tire treads and deer carcasses and stalled cars and rusty mufflers. Every year there seemed to be a new baby along, and eventually there were six kids.

Papa would say, "The snow won't come to you, you have to go to the snow."

We never lost the race. But each year's heroic effort became the stuff of legend, and each year we got a later and later start. That race became such a big part of the trip that I later wondered if Papa hadn't deliberately set off at the last possible minute. I wondered if having more and more kids wasn't designed to increase the level of difficulty. Back then we were three people, four people, five people, six people, seven people, and finally eight people in one station wagon. Now, 30 years later, we were 23 people in seven vehicles.

Georgy whined, "How long's this going to take anyway?" He'd lobbied to stay with his father in Birmingham, mostly because he wanted to maintain his off-season weight-training program with the rest of the muscle-heads on the football team. I had been about Georgy's age for the last Christmas trip to Baraboo, and I vaguely recalled my own adolescent desire to stay home.

Mom fidgeted. She crossed her arms over her chest. She said, "Your Papa went to the doctor." I could tell it was bad news. "His blood pressure's through the roof, his heart's not right, the doctors say they don't even know how he can sit with that back. They said he needs to slow down, to eat better, take some new pills. Lord, I can't keep track of all the pills. Now there's a green kind. Do you know anything about the green kind?" I shrugged. "Then, as you know, he got laid off."

"What did Papa say?"

"He said if you stop you're dead; the thing to do was to always go faster."

The fffffft shook my nervous system like an alarm clock. "We've got 59 hours—that takes into account the time change," Papa said. I turned my hand, ala Vanna White, toward the walkie-talkie: there was Georgy's answer. "We've got to make 26 miles per hour, fffffft, including stops, fffffft, including sleep."

Silence, then static, filled the Alero. Petey had confided in me, back home, that Belinda was going through some bad morning sickness, but nobody was to know about the pregnancy until they got back some test results. "Downs Syndrome runs in her family," he told me. "The last thing we want is to announce a baby's coming, and then there be no baby, if you know what I mean." Then: fffffft. "There's no fat in the schedule," Papa said. "*USA Today* says snow in the Midwest."

The silence, there in the darkness, lasted a while longer, but it seemed, still, as if we were hooked up to the car in front of us, and to the car behind us, and to Papa's voice, which again, after a time, penetrated the early morning stillness.

"I hope everybody got the bathroom out of the way," he said.

We drove the first few hours toward daylight. I loved the serenity at the very start of a trip. The road stretched endlessly ahead, and the symphonic sound of tires rolling, rolling, rolling over I-95's gravel-speckled blacktop deepened the dreamy sensation. You were aware of your body hurtling from one place to another to another, of the vast dimensions of space and time. The blackness turned indigo, gray, hazy blue, then a kind of apricot.

"One Fifty-Eight Point Five." Papa's voice jolted the Alero.

"A dollar fifty-seven back in West Palm Beach," Mom said, holding down the walkie-talkie button longer than necessary. Every time we passed a gas station, either Mom or Papa yelled out the price of unleaded. They compared prices, city-to-city, state-to-state, and chain-to-chain. Georgy rolled his big, black eyes. He said, "I'll pay for the next tank my own self if you guys'll just stop the yammering." I turned my head and

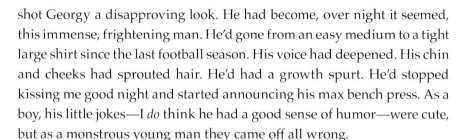

shot Georgy a disapproving look. He had become, over night it seemed, this immense, frightening man. He'd gone from an easy medium to a tight large shirt since the last football season. His voice had deepened. His chin and cheeks had sprouted hair. He'd had a growth spurt. He'd stopped kissing me good night and started announcing his max bench press. As a boy, his little jokes—I *do* think he had a good sense of humor—were cute, but as a monstrous young man they came off all wrong.

"We'll fill up before we cross into Georgia." Ffffffft. "How's every-body doing on fuel?" Ffffffft. "Patsy?"

"Half-tank."

"Find out about Janine."

I relayed the message. "Little more than half."

And so on. Our queue, deliberately or not, was arranged in descend-ing order by age. The middle cars each had two walkie-talkies, one hooked up to the forward car and the other to the backward car. One discount Radio Shack model worked only with its discount Radio Shack mate.

I lobbied for Belinda. "Papa?" FFFTTT. "Belinda's got stomach flu. We have to stop for air every so often and in case she has to throw up."

The walkie-talkie crackled, and Papa said, "There's a place to pull off coming up. We do this one puke stop, and at the same time we fix her up with barf bags. Pass it along."

I relayed. "Belinda's got stomach flu, we're pulling over."

Fingers pressed buttons, and Belinda's delicate condition, though not the real one, got translated to, "Belinda barf break!!!" "Puke stop for Belinda!!!" "We're pulling over so Belinda can vomit!!!"

Florida was a big state, and we needed to slash across it, and then up nearly its length. Over St. Lucie Canal, past Yeehaw Junction and St. Cloud, around Winter Garden, through San Felasco Hammock Preserve, clear up into Jennings. We held a steady course between the Gulf of Mexico and the Atlantic Ocean. I flipped from country station to coun-try station, finally settled on the seductive voice of a radio Evangelist. "Great," Georgy sighed. "Now we're going to listen to some Bible freak for God knows how many miles." He snatched his portable tape player from a bag, slid the earphones over his head, and tuned us out.

I could see Papa's bald spot, awash in morning light, ahead. The U-Haul served as his command center. Papa had maps, coffee, the CB, the walkie-talkie. He had Jack's mobile phone and a radio tuned to an all-weather station. He had snacks and sunglasses and a big stick to adjust the driver's side mirror. His back pills, his heart pills, his cholesterol pills. I think he carried cyanide capsules, in case he was caught behind enemy lines. The Evangelist said, "THE LORD KNOWS."

I'd volunteered, back in West Palm Beach, to share U-Haul driving duties, but Papa had said it was impossible.

"They won't let there be any other driver," he'd said.

"Sure they will, this way you can rest your back some, and be with Mom. I'll go down and give them my driver's license," I'd said.

Papa always had things his way. He introduced unlikely, but hard-to-dispute, evidence into his arguments. "They don't do that, it's about the insurance."

I knew that in the history of people moving their shit across the country, we weren't the first family to want to share driving duties. But Papa wanted to drive the truck and he was going to drive the truck.

Papa always drove back then, too. It wasn't even discussed. Papa retained old-fashiony ideas about gender roles, and would never let a woman drive in his place. The first station wagon I remember was a rusted, dented, hulking Chevy—yellow more than brown—with ripped vinyl in the back seat. Then there was the blue Pontiac with the back seat facing backward, followed by the brand new, paneled Oldsmobile with two sets of back seats. (We always fought to sit in the *back-back*.)

We had one eight-track cassette, *Lynn Anderson's Greatest Hits*, which meant our theme song was, *I Never Promised You a Rose Garden*. But we seldom listened to music. Just after citizen's band radios went from 25 to 40 channels, Papa paid cash for a top-of-the-line unit. He tuned into Channel 19, and left it there for the rest of my childhood.

When the reception on the CB went, Papa would let it crackle and sizzle and moan as he stared at the road over a lit Kent cigarette. I always entertained my brothers and sisters with magic tricks I'd gotten as presents from Grandma and Grandpa Winsconsin. Baraboo was home to

Circus World, and though I'd never been—maybe *because* I'd never been—it held a certain sway over me. I knew I would grow up to be a magician, just as Janine knew she would become a cartoonist and Ruth knew she would be a fashion designer and Petey knew he would be a musician and Jack knew he would be a baseball player and Barry knew he would be whatever Jack was. There in the car, with miles and hours separating us from our destination, we displayed our talents to captive siblings.

I remember once watching Papa slick back his pompadour and thinking it was him against the road.

"Smokey at Mile Marker 131," Papa's voice yelled. "Speed trap just past the viaduct. Step light and let Old Smokey sleep."

We relayed the message. The caravan, bumper-to-bumper-to-et al. hit the brakes. We passed the state trooper. "OKAY," Papa's voice boomed. "CLEAR." The caravan accelerated. I monitored the red speedometer needle as it soared from 65 to 70 to 75 to 80 and settled at 82.

I pressed the button to lobby for poor Belinda. "We need a break, Papa." I pleaded. Ffftt. "Papa, did you hear me?"

"We can't be having tea parties every twenty minutes," Papa shot back.

"It's been three hours."

We pulled into a gas station around Ocala. Janine and Paulo's three boys started chasing each other around the lot. Ruth carried Twin 1 into the bathroom for a change, with Twin 2 next in the queue. Jack's girl bolted for the toys section of the mini mart.

Papa popped the hood, set the gas nozzle on automatic, and yelled, "This ain't recess. We're back on the road in…" He looked at his watch. "Six minutes."

He went from car to car to car, checking oil, cleaning windshields, and filling tires. The last of us returned to the cars. Papa closed shut Jack's portable phone.

"I just talked to your Grandma," Papa said.

"Is she excited about seeing everybody for Christmas?"

"She doesn't know if it's Christmas or the Chinese New Year." He paused. "But I found out from the woman at the front desk, the nursing home does their Christmas dinner at three o'clock, not five o'clock." Papa never out-and-out smiled, but *pleased* was now registered in the Heavenward angle of his pompadour. He relished each setback. He wished every stone in his path might be a boulder. He turned over his watch again. "That gives us two less hours than we'd planned on." He said it in such a way that Grandma's Costly Bungle sounded like "OIL!"

He spread out a map on the warm hood of the Alero. "A trucker told me to avoid the construction zone near where I-10 crosses," he said. "We're going to take 41—it runs parallel to 75 all the way into Georgia—and then cut over on 84 to pick the big road back up. If we get behind a tractor or some old lady out for a Sunday drive…" He stared at the map as if it were a pinwheel slowing, slowing, slowing. Still. "If *I* pass, we *all* have to pass."

"If we late, we late, that's it," Paolo said.

Papa snarled. He attributed Paolo's rich Argentinean accent to pretentiousness. He said, "I had the nursing home set 23 extra places—it's all paid for in advance."

Road mostly still lay ahead, but road did now lie behind. Mom pulled a half-finished knitting project from her bag; she examined a frayed thread in the fuzzy sunshine. I watched Mom out of the corner of one eye, the roadside out the other. I paid attention to the road ahead, Georgy in the backseat, all the cars behind. I fiddled with the radio. Suddenly, I got woozy. My vision became slightly distorted.

Mom dropped her sweater to work the walkie-talkie. "Janine, break for Jan-ine."

"You don't have to say *break*, Granny," Georgy blurted, critically.

I swallowed. My throat felt dry. I sipped orange juice, thinking maybe my blood sugar level was low. I concentrated on the road. This was scaring me. Then, as suddenly as it came, the swooning sensation left.

"You like green, don't you? I mean in clothing? For example, in a turtleneck sweater, for example."

"Yes, Mom," Janine said.

Every Christmas, Mom inadvertently told everybody exactly what they were going to get, almost down to the page number in the Bealls catalogue. Though she had completed all her shopping, and in fact had the wrapped presents stored in the U-Haul, she needed reassurances she'd done okay and so one by one quizzed the other six cars on their Christmas gifts.

"Give Jimmy the walkie," Mom said to the receiver.

"HI, GRANDMA." His tittering echoed through our Alero.

"Jimmy, do you like monster Game Boy cartridges, like, I think there's a Monster Force kind?"

"MIDGE," Papa yelled. "KEEP THE WALKIE-TALKIE CLEAR. We NEED the walkie-talkies CLEAR in case we have something IMPORTANT to say."

Mom stuck out her tongue at the walkie-talkie. "Roger," she said, and forgot to lift her thumb. We were on a two-lane road, and sure enough we got behind a law-abiding spinster in a Honda Accord. Dad decided to take her on the straightaway. Fffffffft. "Okay, Patsy you're fine, Paulo's clear too. Nothing but road." Being two-deep on the wrong side of the road at 90 miles an hour felt strangely exciting and dangerous; it must have been even more so for the cars behind.

The sky, the weather, had yet to change. The impending snowstorm secretly thrilled Papa (THREE CHERRIES!), and all the kids; me, too, I'll have to admit. I experienced, for the first time since I was a child, the anticipation of change. The moving landscape—it always seemed as though it and not us were in motion—retained a yellowing and tan aspect. But looking at the speedometer—86 miles per hour—I knew that wouldn't last.

"PULL OVER." The words boomed out of our walkie-talkie, and when I checked the rearview mirror there was a procession of walkie-talkies held to mouths. The message, relayed to me via Barry, Jack, Peter, Ruth and finally Janine, was: "Peter's got a blown back tire." I notified Papa. He eased the U-Haul to the shoulder. I pulled the Alero behind. Soon, all seven cars idled off to the side of the road. We opened our doors after one car and before another car zoomed past. Papa rubbed his hands together. "Blown tire," he said, as if it were "TAX REBATE!" He riffled through

Petey's trunk, grabbed a spare tire, grabbed a jack, jacked the car up, lay down on his bad back: a one-man pit crew.

"There's bushes down there." Papa pointed with the wrench. "Anybody's got to go, go now." We took turns peeing behind the bush, as Papa and the boys fixed the tire. Mom continued her interviews. "Jason, you always need socks, don't you always need socks, like the orange and blue Gator socks?"

In a brief time, Papa clapped his hands together, wiped grease off on a rag, then looked at his watch. "27 minutes," he reported. "We lost 27 minutes."

"Now entering The Peach State," the walkie-talkie boomed. I looked up. We all looked up. State line crossings were always, in our childhood trips, treated with reverence, a watershed moment and proof we were Making Time. There were usually five, depending on our route: Georgia, Tennessee, Kentucky, Illinois and finally Wisconsin.

Billboards hawked Pebble Hill Plantation, Stephen Foster Folk Culture Center, Jefferson Davis Memorial, Six Flags, Atlanta Motor Speedway, Georgia Cotton Museum, Kennesaw Mountain Battlefield, and Etowah Mounds. Some decrepit white billboards merely advertised, "Available." We sped past these places along the way. I stared at the rolling scenery, but after a while it seemed sedentary. Our lives are like that, everything seems top speed during childhood, and then our bodies, our minds, slow down, and it surprises us, looking back, there's all this road behind us.

As the day wore on, it became harder and harder to stay on the road. The twins were teething. Petey's wife Belinda had a touch of the stomach flu. Angie's throat was on fire: early stages of tonsillitis. Mom's hemorrhoids were acting up. I experienced another hot flash, then another. It was terribly discomforting, puzzling, and for reasons I couldn't explain, even to myself, embarrassing.

Then Barry got diarrhea. If having diarrhea wasn't its own punishment, Barry had also to endure the message being relayed over seven vehicles. Fffffft. "Barry's got the runs!!" Fffffft. "We need to pull over:

Barry can't hold it." Fffffft. "Montezuma's Revenge!!!" Ffffffftt. "Barry is going to crap his pants."

"The shits!" Dad said into the walkie-talkie, in a tone that signified, "STRAIGHT FLUSH!"

It was a traveling Bodily Fluids Release show. We stopped a bunch of times. With all our vehicles and all our kids and all our minor ailments, these weren't, could not be, mere pit stops.

That first day, I struggled to keep going. It felt like fatigue and yet not fatigue, exactly. We weren't quite to Tennessee. The tawny landscape, off-set with patches of rust and green, became suffused with rose at sunset. The bare trees, and the odd evergreen, looked epic against the dramatic twilight. The tired farm machinery seemed that much more dignified. As night pushed out day, the pattern of lights—taillights, roadside reflectors, roadside houses, street lights, service stations—changed into ignomini-ous shapes. A peninsula running perpendicular to the road. A lighthouse. Falling trees. I controlled my panic and tried to stare through the dancing elves to the curve in the road, past the stampeding reindeer to the lane closure. I found Papa's taillights for support, the only absolutely true thing I could depend on.

The neighborhoods along the highway lit up with Christmas. Through our blurred glimpses, the houses seemed beautiful and bright. Papa naturally wanted to push farther, deep into blackness, but, finally, berated for miles by the walkie-talkie, assented to stop early. When we checked into the hotel, Papa stood in the parking lot. He looked at the sky. "We're behind schedule," he said. "Way behind schedule." Mom touched his elbow to urge him inside.

Mom and Papa were going on 48 years married. Mom had seen him at the gas station on a spring morning in 1954 and knew. She didn't have a driver's license, so Sally Wakefield borrowed Old Man Wakefield's Cadillac. Mom and Sally drove there, sometimes twice a day, for fifty cents' worth.

"He looked just like Elvis then," Mom liked to say. Papa always retort-ed, "Elvis looked just like me."

Papa tilted his face skyward. His pompadour dated back to his ado-lescence, though it was considerably thinned and streaked with silver.

He still had the single cigarette behind one ear, even though he hadn't smoked in a decade. The ever-present scent of Hi-Karate cologne lingered. Everything was reasonably the same and somehow completely different. He rolled up the sleeves of his short sleeve shirt. It was a near-freezing night in Cartersville, Georgia, our first stopping place. Even in West Palm Beach, winter nights could get down near freezing but almost always stopped well short of snow conditions.

"14 hours, 650 miles," Papa said. He shook his head: not good enough.

"We'll be fine," I said. "Less than 900 miles in two days, no problem." I always said it would be fine, whether I thought it would be fine or not. It was something I inherited from Mom: wanting, desperately, to make people feel better. I'd thought sometimes that it was so much fecklessness, but in more magnanimous moments chalked it up to a kind spirit.

"A day and a half," Dad reminded.

"Can we please just get there so we can get it over with?" Georgy, that ungrateful monster of mine, wheezed.

A bundled-up couple—apparently coming from north to south—rolled a suitcase toward us. They stopped. "Did you hear yet?" the man asked.

"Hear what?" Dad asked.

"We just beat it. Big blizzard on the way. They're calling it The Storm of The Century."

"Storm of the Century?" Papa repeated, as if it were, "UNEXPECTED INHERITANCE!" "I knew *snow*, but I didn't hear *Storm of the Century*."

"That's what they're saying." The couple disappeared into the hotel lobby.

Papa studied the sky. The tiny, brilliant stars twinkled against a deep, dark canvas. In all our years in West Palm Beach, we'd only seen a smattering of snowflakes and never the out-and-out snowstorm we were driving into now. Snowball fights and snowmen and snow angels came in a collage of Baraboo Christmas memories. All of us, from Grandma Winsconsin to Papa and Mom, to all my siblings and second and third cousins, to my aunts and uncles, remained, in my memory, a fixed age that must have been our ages around the end of the Disco Era.

"The thing about a snowstorm…" Papa reached for his unlit cigarette, and in a single motion shifted it from behind his ear to the side of his mouth. "It's only good if you're already parked. Otherwise…" He shook his head. He closed his eyes and sniffed the night air. "We're on a collision course. We're going to the snow and the snow's coming to us."

A gold crucifix rested on Papa's wrinkled, burnt chest. A red oil rag hung from his back pocket. Despite the chilly conditions he wore short sleeves and left his top three shirt buttons undone.

"We'll have to get an earlier jump tomorrow, and drive longer."

"How's your back?" I asked.

"Don't worry about my back," he said.

Mom touched Papa's shoulder again. I noticed Jack peeking out from his hotel window. Belinda had disappeared, and I knew we wouldn't see her again until morning. Barry retreated, emaciated, to a chair within striking distance of the toilet. We all showed visible signs of fatigue, all but Papa. He looked wired, he looked determined, he looked like a man who knew only victory.

The sky, that second day, changed to a dreary gray and the air turned dense. It started to drizzle. Everything in our path was wet and cold and somber. We contended with the backwash from trucks and other cars, but mostly from our own family caravan. A one or two degrees temperature drop would turn all that rain into snow, all the water into ice, and that was what we were fighting: one or two degrees. We were crossing the Georgia border into Chattanooga, Tennessee, The Storm of the Century ever looming on the horizon.

Janine announced that she, too, had stomach flu, and speculated that she'd gotten it from Belinda. Barry, gaunt and beaten, asked once, twice, three times to stop at rest stops. Over the walkie-talkie, his apologetic voice said, "I'm sorry…"

Ruth's husband Sebastian proposed we wait out the storm in a Hilton. We only stayed at mid-range chain hotels located right off an exit ramp: Day's Inn, Comfort Inn, Howard Johnson's, Budget Inn. The high-end places were, in Papa's mind, too expensive, and the low-end places not good enough.

Papa responded, via the walkie-talkie, "Ffffft...I don't think you can even get a U-Haul into that parking lot."

I'm not sure how Papa concluded that the Hilton was impenetrable by moving truck.

Sebastian responded, "Fffffft....Of course you can. There's no roof; what's stopping you?"

"They don't allow them. They're not allowed."

We pushed on. Barry took over driving for me while Janine took over for him. Some of the cousins switched cars to be with favorite cousins. Wives and husbands traded places. Changing the deck made it seem, for a brief time, like a brand new game. Our car got assigned Weather Conditions updates. There was constant communication between cars regarding Travel Advisories while we flew past trees and pastures, sailed by mile markers and crumbling barns, whizzed over rivers and under freight trains.

The storm sounded like a bad one. I thought Dad should push forward with the U-Haul, and maybe one car should follow; the indisposed and immature among us should wait out the weather. Dad said, "There's no way we could unload and get set up without the extra hands. Besides, this family sticks together."

I sat in the back with Juan. I went to my old bag of tricks. I fanned the cards out, "Pick a card, any card." I changed a red thimble to a blue thimble. I made a quarter vanish into my elbow.

Strips of snow lined highway embankments. My headache, partly due to Motrin, was in remission, but I dreaded what now seemed inevitable: this frightening spell happening again, and again.

"How did you do it?" Juan cried. I wouldn't say. Even though I'd long ago given up magic, I held to the sacred trust. Without mystery, there is no magic.

"One Forty Eight, Daniel," Mom shrieked from the front seat.

"You have to release the button, Mom," Barry said.

"Release THE BUTTON, Midge," Papa's voice yelled.

We stopped that second night, Christmas Eve, 315 miles short of Baraboo. We'd gone a tad more than 550 miles in a smidgen better than 14 hours, meaning our pace had slowed considerably. We bowed our

heads in the Red Barn Buffet in Tuscola, Illinois. Dad said a blessing. We amened amidst the chaos of an Amish family-style restaurant's clattering and clanking. We still had a shot at making dinner tomorrow, but we'd have to pierce The Storm to get there. "Straight to bed, everybody," Papa said. "We start early."

"How early?" Jack asked.

"Early early," Papa said.

I was driving somewhere near Bloomington, Illinois, when the first gorgeous white shavings miraculously settled on our windshield. My forehead felt damp, real damp, and my vision blurred, bad. It was now a full-body pain—intense, almost overwhelming. I checked the back seat, where a heavy bass line thrummed from the general vicinity of Georgy's closed eyes and slumping head. The windshield wipers swish, swish, swished away, and for a second I didn't think I could go on.

I'd had trouble sleeping lately and lacked all focus. I had headaches with some regularity, and I'd never before had headaches. The symptoms were there, but I was only 46 years old, too young, surely. I asked Mom, "When did you go through menopause?"

"Oh," Mom said, emphatic. "Oh. Oh. Hot flashes?"

"Something like that," I said. "How old?"

"It happened a little early for me. Your age."

I regretted having confided in Mom, of all people, but it also relieved my mind, in a way. I was scared and needed somebody else to know. *Menopause.* God, was I truly an old person myself? I thought back on my life—a failed marriage, a series of jobs that hardly constituted a career, a son who would soon no longer need me—and wondered a little what it all added up to.

Mom's finger twittered on the walkie-talkie button. I dripped sweat. My hair felt damp, my sweater strangled me. Through a bright swirl of colors, I saw Mom's finger push down the button, and then her voice wafted through my clouds. "Patricia is going through her Change of Life," Mom yelled.

The family's voices thrummed through the Alero. "The Change!... She's turning Saint Catherine's corner....Pat's Entering Midlife....HOT FLASHES. We have to STOP."

We were succumbing to the enemy. We were back on the road, but things had suddenly turned wet, white and dangerous. Snow pounded. You got the feeling that, for the snow, there was no turning back, like troops overtaking a city. We pushed on, and pushed on, but there was too much weather and too much sickness from too many directions. Traffic all but stopped. Cars eased along the highway, and us, a caravan of seven, had no choice but to go as slow as the slowest of them. The red speed-ometer plunged to barely 10 and stayed there. We rode the brakes all the way from Minonk to Love's Park. Every mile or so, we'd see another car rolled over in the center median, or turned completely around in the ditch. People were stopping to help people. At first, the walkie-talkies got a workout. "Stalled car ahead, ease around it on the left..." "Ice patch on the bridge, keep off the brakes..." "No shoulder ahead, stay on the road." Then it fell silent as we poured all our energy and concentration into see-ing the red reflecting lights just ahead of us. We kept within ten yards of each other—enough space so that if one car stopped it wouldn't be a pileup but close enough to provide a beacon. Nobody but Papa thought we should go on, but even though it was 22-1 against, we followed.

It got to where we were the only cars left on the road. Even the salt trucks weren't this nuts. It was mid-day and pitch dark when we hit the Welcome to Wisconsin: America's Dairyland sign. "FFFFFFFT.... WISCONSIN!!!!" penetrated our car. In the background, through the walkie-talkie, I heard triumphant giggles. Under normal conditions, it was an hour and a half to Baraboo, hardly anything, but at our speed it was an almost unreachable distance.

"FFFFFFFT. Get off at the next exit." It was Papa. As we rolled, ever so carefully, onto the exit ramp, I saw up ahead what Papa had seen first: ROAD CLOSED. We assembled in the Visitor's Center parking lot. We were the only cars. I parked and leaped out, slipped and slid to the dark-ened building. I brought my face close to the frosty glass. Nobody there.

The others unraveled. My brothers and sisters, my son, all my nieces and nephews popped out of vehicles. There we were, Christmas Day, stranded at a rest stop with no hope of making dinner. Papa had lost the race. I don't think any of us quite knew how to feel. Mixed with the despair and panic of being stuck, was the exhilaration and calm of being there. We weren't where we wanted to be but we were somewhere.

Papa rubbed his back. He walked over to the abandoned Visitor's Center, tugged at the door, which tugged back. He released the handle, defeated. Mom touched his elbow. "Everything's in the truck," she said. "At least we got everything in the truck."

There was so much snow. It was all glistening and white, and the way it piled high, to our thighs almost, was a miracle. "We'll call Highway Patrol, but nobody's going to clear the road until the snow stops," Papa said.

The Visitor's Center was a square brick and glass building. Inside sat silent racks of tourist pamphlets, a small gift shop, a snack kiosk, and a series of round tables with plastic chairs. Presumably, all these road-side workers were home with their own families, embarking on cozy Christmas days with crinkled wrapping paper, blazing fires and gravy poured indiscriminately over turkey and mashed potatoes.

"We can't even get inside," Ruth said. "Everything's closed up."

We *were* stopped. We were *not* dead. "These locks won't hold us," I said.

All of us became something other than what we were sure we would become. But what we became was only a small part of who we were. Barry, after running to the bathroom, shoveled out the door. I picked the lock. Papa stooped in the back of the U-Haul, sifting through the family's worldly belongings to isolate Christmas gifts, as well as decorations from a box marked, "Christmas." Georgy, Paul Bunyon-like, single-handedly carried stuff from the U-Haul inside, where Fiona hurriedly, and with great panache, decorated the room. Mom and Janine, with my help, broke into the kitchen and started cooking. Ruth set about lighting candles throughout the Visitor's Center café. Sebastian assembled the artificial tree, while Jack fixed strings of lights and Petey dribbled cotton balls on the floor.

The kids ran and played in the snow, then Belinda dried them off and helped them change. We dragged Papa's Chair into the Visitor's Center. "What about Grandma Winsconsin?" Petey asked.

We dialed the nursing home. After a time, Grandma Winsconsin was summoned. We set the phone down and yelled, "Merry Christmas!!!" Dad told her we'd be there after the storm.

Mom giggled as she lowered her old, arthritic body to the floor. She said, "Oh, okay, To: Georgy, From: Grandma and Grandpa."

Georgy opened the Crimson Tide jersey he knew he would get, and I was so proud when he fixed an astonished look on his face and said, "Wow! A Crimson Tide jersey. Thank you, Grandma. Thank you, Grandpa." Then he went over and gave Mom a kiss on the cheek, and despite his muscular, manly body I could see the kid in him again.

Mom shuffled through the pile and found another present. "Oh, okay, To: Janine, From: Mom and Papa." Janine opened the green turtleneck sweater she knew she would get and gasped in shock. "How did you know, Mom? It's perfect."

We went on like that, all of us getting the exact present we knew we would get and acting, to the best of our abilities, as if we were pleasantly surprised. The kids, bless them, gave us adults reclaimable presents, like a framed Winnie-the-Pooh print, and each other sharable gifts, like a chocolate Santa. The kids were giddy. Mom appeared pleased with herself. My brothers and sisters joined me, I believe, in feeling that whatever we'd gone through to bring us to this point wasn't sacrifice but something entirely joyful.

Outside, the sun burst through naked silvery tree branches with the tiny hope of a fortune cookie. I sensed in Papa's face, as he sat there in an unbuttoned short sleeve shirt, more pride than disappointment.

Soon, the roads would be plowed and the way would be relatively safe to travel. But we were in no great hurry now to get on with it, not really.

Almost

There were no slamming bodies, no screams, no squealing brakes or squirting blood, no panic, not even a jolt. We just stopped.

Us passengers on the Pacific Surfliner stretched, shifted, stood up and sat down, the whole time sneaking peeks at fellow holiday travelers. It was Christmas morning.

Officially, Lyle and I had broken up, but I knew that wasn't the bottom line. He had demanded I bring him home. I had refused. We had hurled insults, mapped out faults, presented accusations, and generally unknotted three years of love and affection. "Three years," he kept saying, waving most of one hand in the air. "Three years, Jeremy."

Christmas had brought us to this; Christmas could put us right again.

"They could at least tell you what's going on; it's always some bullshit with them," the guy swaddled in Clippers gear said.

"This is typical," a mother nursing twins said.

"Every time," a man with a black vest and turquoise jewelry added.

Whoever said "Getting there's half the fun" had no idea what they were talking about. We were the poorest of poor travelers—large, bawling families, black sheep sons, struggling artist types. Me: a homosexual horticulturalist. We'd traded comfort, speed and promptness for a tiny savings. Now: this.

Over the muffled, antiquated public address system, a voice announced, "We're experiencing an emergency." *Experiencing*. Like a movie. Or Thai food. A monster truck rally.

A collective groan howled like a dust storm. We were stuck between Ocean City and Solana Beach, no more than five minutes from our penultimate stop. We were tired, anxious, and bored.

"Here we go," the nursing mother said.

"Every time," the turquoise guy repeated.

A stalled boxcar, on a rail just a foot and a half from my own train's rail, blocked both my window view and my sun. Our delay was its delay. The purplish wall of rusty steel loomed before me like a gigantic doodle pad on which to record all my monumental thoughts. Ahead: my judgmental, unsuspecting family. Behind: my estranged, disappointed lover.

Lyle was older than me by a couple of years, which at that age seemed a lot, and he had ensconced himself in a San Francisco neighborhood that not only accepted but expected his homosexuality. He was kind and fiercely intelligent and confident, and our relationship had from the beginning been that of teacher and student. He had wavy black hair and sudsy brown eyes. His lips always remained slightly parted, as if, like an infielder on the balls of his feet, he were prepared to answer back on reflex. I had dabbled in other male, as well as female, affairs, but this was the first that had an adult intensity.

"You are who you are," he said. "You're Jeremy. If your people don't love you for that, or even in spite of that, then that's *their* problem."

I'd started the previous evening on an inland route and transferred to this coastal train in San Luis Obispo. Mist hung over the ocean like a sweet specter and waves rolled on and on. I'd almost stayed there: it seemed such a lovely place to cower. I'd heard somewhere that San Luis Obispo had an annual sidewalk-painting festival, and as I waited for my next train I imagined myself a kneeling Picasso swirling avocado and pink and fuchsia toward harmony. I wondered how many years the sidewalk painting had gone on, and how long before they ran out of sidewalks.

A blue-and-white-suited black man sprinted down the aisle holding his billed cap. I rolled my head. The conductor's black shoes hit the floor and his walkie-talkie rattled. An urgent voice mumbled something unintelligible, and then repeated the indecipherable message.

"What now?" a dowdy brunette whined. "Anybody catch that?"

I grew up thinking love made you happy, despite all evidence to the contrary. My father worked in a golf ball manufacturing plant; he made millions of balls for a sport he would never play. My mom raised us three kids. They slept together every night, I knew that, but I'd never once seen them touch. My dad worked hard—he made barely a living wage without overtime, but there was always plenty of overtime. He raised us children in a series of fortune cookie-like pronouncements that he firmly believed. He said, "You're only as good as your worst thought." And, "You should never worry *too* much, only just enough."

A man stepped into the aisle, then the woman seated beside him. Others rose. With a fire, or an accident on your block, everybody knew exactly where to gather—behind the emergency vehicles' barricade, or in a neighbor's front yard. The rallying point of this tragedy was less clear.

The voice sounded again. "There's been a collision at the crossroads. There will be a delay." Even the patient passengers now groaned. A tiny balled-up fist jabbed my back through the vinyl; the other tiny balled-up fist followed. Two tiny feet kicked.

A man in a cowboy hat yelled, "Donkey's ass!!!"

A woman's irate voice said, "How long's this going to take? They don't even tell you how long it's going to take."

The thought of losing Lyle scared me, but I also felt that maybe I should gamble on happy. "You'll never be happy," Lyle had declared. "Until you can be proud of who you are."

Before the sex, we'd been friends, or friends of friends, and we used to crank call Miss Mary Muffins. It was always the same: we'd listen on speakerphone as a gigantic sounding, cigarette-smoking black man would answer, "Miss Mary Muffins." We'd hold back laughter and ask for the specials, and he would hack them out. "Chipper Chocolate. Purr-fect Pecan. Heavenly Hot Chocolate." The voice was deep, gruff and out-of-joint, like a spurned Barry White, or a depressed Louie Armstrong. We imagined some prissy, zealous housewife hiring this boxer or bluesman to help run her muffin business. We pictured him towering over a blackboard busy with hearts and cute inspirational sayings. We often threatened to visit Miss Mary Muffins, but never did; I think it would have ruined our fun to actually know, rather than imagine, the place.

I remembered another of my dad's pronouncements: "Don't get sidetracked by happy."

A slinking, shirking little tanned man took it upon himself to play Columbo. He stroked his graying mustache, straightened his wilted collar, and hiked up his black socks. "I'll see what I can find out," he announced to nobody special. He was gone.

The dim train retained the smells it had picked up all the way down the line: Grover Beach, Lompoc, Santa Barbara, Carpinteria, Ventura, Oxnard, Simi Valley, Van Nuys, Burbank Airport, Fullerton, Anaheim, Santa Ana, Irvine, San Juan Capistrano, San Clemente, and Oceanside. Did I retain some of Lyle's smell: Hugo Boss toilette spray, Clearin or after-gardening sweat? Had Lyle awoken this morning smelling of the rich lathery decadence of a Christmas Eve night out in the Tenderloin district?

My family did not expect me, not today. I had originally intended to spend Christmas Day with Lyle and travel home the next day. I hadn't even called for a ride. I silently rehearsed a speech I would deliver to the whole family as we gathered around the Christmas tree. I would volunteer to pass out presents—that would give me the stage— and as my father, mother, siblings, aunts, uncles and cousins stared at me, rapt with Christmas glee, drowsy from Christmas ham, exhausted from Christmas preparations, I'd clear my throat. I'd say, "I have an announcement." As I mentally looked into each pair of eyes, I could see only shock, confusion, dismay and anger; no understanding. We were a family of Republican-voting, minority-hating homophobics who snapped off the TV set when images of gay or mixed-marriage couples appeared, editorializing, without dissent, about society's responsibility to scourge such diseased people from the planet. Nobody, save my mom, would ever love me the same.

It wasn't just Lyle. It was my job, my home, everything. I'd given up my swimming scholarship and transferred colleges, and I'd switched majors in the process. I went from history to horticulture. I thought in the future I'd study architecture, interior design, more history—I wanted to buy, fix up and sell beautiful homes. But when I graduated, the best job I could find was in a Christmas tree factory. I was in charge of a bunch of Hispanic housewives, our mission to arrange bows and ribbons and do-dads around fir branches. There were five pre-packaged design variations that we executed over and over. It was the kind of commercial enterprise I loathed, and I fretted constantly over the fact that there wasn't much difference between Dad's golf balls and my Christmas trees.

Columbo, Jr. returned. He waved his gnarled left hand with a flourish. "It's the way I figured," he said. "There's been a death; that makes this a crime scene. The police have to clear the area—for us that means we have to stay put. A complete investigation is what they have to do. I'm still talking to somebody on the staff, getting all the low-down."

"Was it a car?" somebody asked.

"Personally, that's what I think," he said, and raised a knowing gray eyebrow. "Here's what I can tell you: they're reopening the lounge car." He said it as though it were a concession he'd won. "Give it a few minutes, then go down there and load up. What they have left is what they have left."

I could look *through* the glass at the purple boxcar, or I could look *at* the glass at layered reflections. Fellow passengers projected as distant, tiny images—in fact, I could, with concentration, position them on outer tracks or even the hills. The reflections seemed to double back on each other to form a whole village of obscured heads: heads reading papers, heads jotting notes, heads talking, heads napping. I followed telephone wires, cables, poles, a giant radio antenna; the sheer infrastructure was daunting.

A woman's tiny, squeaky voice declared, "No matter if the guard's down or not, you have to slow down to look. I always look, just to make sure."

How could she be so certain it could not have been her? How could any of us?

A lower-pitched woman's voice whined, "We need some air. It's not funny: we need air in here."

There was no power, meaning no ventilation system. All the windows and doors were closed. People talked and stretched. The train buzzed with low chatter. Passengers came back from the lounge car with cheese Danishes and muffins, pretzels and Sprite. We still knew only what Columbo, Jr. had told us, but speculation was wild and fairly specific.

Somebody in a hurry, probably on their way to meet somebody, or late for work. That's still no excuse.

Kids. They do it for fun. Race the train. Well, now they've had their fun.

They thought it was a freight train; got surprised when the passenger train came through.

"No coffee," somebody announced. "Forget about the coffee."

A small man with a big head re-emerged from the lounge car. "I'm only staying in San Diego two days to begin with," he sighed. "By the time I get there, I'm going to have to fucking turn around and come home."

The Clippers fan commiserated. "Tell me about it: I got an uncle in town all the way from New York; he's gonna be gone before I get there."

"No beer," somebody reported.

"No more sandwiches."

I kept thinking about that town with all the painted sidewalks: there must have been beautiful, elaborate murals, colorful cartoons, and children's tender farm animal renderings. Did everybody walk heads down everywhere they went? Surely, I could lose myself in a place like that, without all the drama and heartbreak I now faced. Why, anyway, did I have to *declare* who or what I was? Wasn't it up to others to *discover* that? It did not seem fair that my sexual orientation counted so much more than that of a heterosexual—that my interests, ambitions, accomplishments, my generosity and kindness, my humility and open-mindedness meant nothing compared to the fact that I liked men.

Whose business was it anyway? Whose fucking business?

"No more muffins." "No more nachos." The hard liquor ran out, then the orange juice.

A worker opened a door between cars, then stood, arms crossed, guarding the exit. The fresh, cold air slowly filled the car. People tried to look around the train worker toward the length of tracks where the accident had happened. Emergency vehicles drove alongside the train. Ambulances, squad cars, tow trucks—flashing lights and siren songs played against the backdrop of the green hills.

"It's 80 dollars less if you travel on Christmas; that's how they suck you in," the nursing mother said.

"I got a coupon, the kids they ride two for one," said a mom. "The airlines charge you full fare."

"It ain't worth the aggravation," somebody cautioned.

Christmas Day ticked away. People had probably gone to the moon in less time than it would take us to traverse the state of California. This wasn't so much leisurely travel as a hostage situation in which the captors had no demands for our safe return. I tried to sleep, but Lyle, my parents, and those dead kids haunted my dreams. Were they really racing the train, or absent-mindedly looking for a store open on Christmas Day? "Don't get your hopes up on the pretzels." Was the driver consumed with joyous or stressful Christmas thoughts? "Water's gone now, too; they're closing the lounge car again." Did it matter?

A conductor stepped into our car, shaking his head. "Almost made it," he said. He shook his head again. He told us that two teenagers were dead, two others in critical condition. "They were halfway across; panicked and hit the brakes when the whistle blew. Al-most." He said it as though those teenagers were the underdogs all along.

"Even if you for some reason don't see the gate, you can hear that clanging for miles."

"What do you expect when you race the train?"

The overwhelming consensus was: those dead and seriously injured people had fucked up our Christmas Day.

Columbo, Jr., returned with a follow-up report. "One of the cars got unhooked; that's got to be fixed, too. They're not even going to try and get us all the way to San Diego. Once they get us to Solana Beach, there'll be buses waiting."

I closed my eyes. I lulled myself to sleep creating sidewalks: I did a cityscape, a robin, a clown, a head and shoulders of Lyle smiling, a Victorian House, an English village, my family's portrait. I tried to make each sidewalk creation represent an important aspect of my life, and speculated on how many sidewalks would be erased in the fallout from my announcement. I dreamt of today, or an imaginary today. Though this dream was set on Christmas Day, it had the texture of a time both immediate and long ago. In this dream, a somewhat distant friend of the family's, a man I'd met two or three times, but not since before I hit puberty, was my dad. My mom was my mom. They were both preoccupied with a million household chores, and as I announced my homosexuality they "uh-huhed" and nodded without pausing, as though I'd reported a drippy faucet or said the pie smelled good. I awoke. My dream snapped. Here I was, hoping not for shared jubilation, just indifference, and yet it was a ridiculous fantasy.

It was late afternoon. I looked at my watch, nearly four o'clock, or eight hours behind schedule. A train worker announced he was opening the other side door. "Nobody is to leave the train," he threatened. The metal squeaked, and the sun and air had a dazzling, life-affirming effect that seemed to improve the train's mood.

I was aware, like everybody else, I assume, of my fellow passengers' movements, and I watched out of the corner of my eye as a little Chinese woman struggled to open a tin of sardines. It required a can opener, which she apparently didn't have. Her squinched-up, spotted, barium yellow face indicated she did not speak English. The Clippers fanatic reached into his sagging jeans and produced a pocketknife; he offered it to the little Chinese woman. She nodded, took the knife, and proceeded to poke at the tin with little result. The college girl next to me, who had slept through 17 stops, two deaths, two critical injuries and hours of idleness, had now awoken but still looked extremely fatigued. She pulled a Banana Slug keychain corkscrew from a knapsack and held it up for

the little Chinese woman to see. The little Chinese woman handed the tin to the sleepy college girl, who worked three earnest but unsuccessful minutes at opening it. She handed the tin to me, and I studied it, scraped at it with a key, and then gave it to an outstretched hand, which began its assault with a box cutter. "I got it started," the man connected to the arm announced, and relayed the sardine tin to a woman with knitting needles. The little Chinese woman looked appreciatively on, twinkling a thin thanks to each failed savior. The sardine tin made its way through our car—passengers pried it open with eyeglass screwdrivers, flattened coins, souvenir bookmarks. Finally, the Clippers fanatic got another shot and popped the lid. "Got her," he said, and triumphantly handed the tin to the grateful little Chinese woman. She bowed, and handed the Clippers fanatic a napkin before motioning for him to take a sardine. He did. The little Chinese woman turned to the sleepy college girl, shook a napkin toward her, and then held out the tin. Some passengers passed but many accepted; slimy silver sardines slid down our throats. We gulped. The tin boomeranged back to the little Chinese woman, who ate her last sardine as if it were plenty.

Columbo, Jr. charged into our car. "It's like this: there's damage to the engine car. They don't know if it can be patched up or if it has to be towed."

I began to nod off again, but was startled to by a yank and an "Oh, my God!!!" I looked as my purplish wall slid an inch or two, a few inches more, until I could read large white-stenciled letters that said, "Built in Oregon by Gunderson."

"We're going back," somebody yelled. "Are we going back?"

"I don't know where we're going, but we're making better time."

"Why are we going back?"

"Jesus Christ!"

I stared at the purplish wall. It moved slowly, and stopped. Moved slowly, and stopped. All of a sudden, a city street bathed in sunlight revealed itself through a space above a low, flatbed trailer. It appeared out of nowhere, like another car's bumper at a hidden stop sign. It was just a normal neighborhood, but greenish and alive with Christmas. The wind blew a piece of paper high into air and then released it; I followed its slow descent onto a lawn decorated with cardboard cutout Christmas packages. We inched beyond the crack and stalled next to another purplish steel railroad car. When we moved again, I glimpsed a lighted wire silhouette of Father Christmas.

It took us forever but we finally reversed all the way into the Oceanside station. A long queue formed behind the solitary pay phone. Passengers dropped in change and hurriedly, excitedly reported that they were okay, that they'd be home before Christmas ended. A bus to San Diego would leave in twenty minutes. Passengers continued to assure loved ones that everything was all right, and as I waited my turn I considered who were my loved ones and whether everything *was* all right. I could count my family as loved ones only if I continued my deception and Lyle as a loved one only if I ended it. Nobody, anyhow, suspected anything was wrong. When it came my turn, I dialed Miss Mary Muffins—I'd long since memorized the number—but instead of the gruff, smoky black man's voice, I heard a sweet, recorded, white woman's voice chirp, "Merry Christmas! Miss Mary's Muffins is closed for the holidays. Please call back after December 26."

I replaced the receiver. I moved toward the bus, slowly, cautiously. This was the way it was: despite all the plans and forecasts and promises, we'd get there when we got there.

His Side of the Family

We consummated our fledgling relationship in a concrete wigwam two days before Christmas. Theodore Morganfield crashed into me (*I love you, Claire*), retreated, crashed into me (*I never felt this way*), retreated. I thrashed (*I love you, Teddy*) and wriggled (*You're so amazing*), and we both whimpered and groaned and tugged, and our frightful shadows danced with us on three sloping walls. Then: panting. Then: complete silence.

It had taken three months of daily phone calls to carefully negotiate, plan and stage this eight-minute event. We lay there in a sweaty, prickly heap. I wondered, staring at the apex where there would have been a ceiling: *my future husband?* We'd been apart all but two days of the three months we'd known each other—he there in Cave City, Kentucky, me in my hometown of St. Louis, Missouri. Didn't matter. I insisted on being married, and at 23 I already felt old. I wanted not only a husband, but children (two girls, one boy), a house in the suburbs, and volunteer work with the local library and PTA, in that order. Horse riding lessons could come later. Everything I did, everything I thought about, was related to that end goal.

"Wow," Teddy said. "Wow. Wow." Each *wow* lost a little steam. I knew from past experience that *post-coital* could be defined as, "I take back everything I said until just now." I was trying to get a read.

"Yes," I said. I told myself I didn't want to be too aggressive—even though we *had* ravaged each other over the phone and just now in the flesh. I didn't want to be coy, either. "Wonderful."

We lay on our backs, my left hand entwined in Teddy's right hand, his meaty right leg flopped over my bony left leg. He said, his words climbing toward the room's Indianesque point, "Claire, I believe if two people are totally honest with each other then they'll always tell the truth."

I couldn't disagree. Teddy's confessional tone made me peek over at him. He had that slumped look insincere men get after they've had an orgasm. It wasn't just sleepiness, though certainly there was that. He seemed like a boy at a carnival who'd hit the center of the star and saw no reason to throw another dart.

He went on to tell me that every time he fell in love with a woman, he became convinced she was the only woman he could ever love, until—usually about three months into the thing—he met another woman whom he became convinced was the only woman he could ever love. By way of example, he mentioned Phyllis, who, technically speaking, he'd been seeing the night we met in St. Louis and for "a spell" after that. In Teddy's opinion, his honesty in this matter excused his behavior, and anyway he felt his past lovers had been satisfied and happy right up to that certain point. "That's still a doggone lot of happy, even if you count what came later." He added, "But I don't think me and you are like that." He paused. "Then again, that's what I always think."

I withdrew my chalky miniature fingers from his greasy super-sized fingers. I should have been angry, but I was biologically predisposed to substitute self-doubt for rage. I said I wasn't interested in a short, powerful affair. I wanted a man who wanted something permanent. It gave me some pleasure to match Teddy blunt-for-blunt. He took back my fingers. "That's good," he said. "I'm not a betting man, but I bet you we last."

Men baffled me. I suppose the "There's somebody else" speech got easier with practice. But so many other methods seemed easier. Casual dating. Self-control. An open relationship. Old-fashioned monogamy.

Worse than consummating an affair in a concrete wigwam was spending the night there alone. Teddy said there was no way around it. "Mine's a church-going family," Teddy said, "so I fudged the timeline a bit. They think you get here tomorrow." He would pick me up in the morning, as if from the airport.

Christmas in Cave City. Teddy loved everything about his home-town—he loved the weather, he loved the people, he loved the caves and he loved The Cats, he loved the concrete wigwams. When he told me about Cave City, I felt like an obnoxious tourist, but when he invited me there I felt like a welcomed guest. We'd talked about marriage in the abstract. Teddy had said he wanted "little ones." As always, I got worked up: this might be, could be, *it*.

Teddy popped up. He stood on the bed, gathering clothes. He hovered, naked, above me. "Yes sir," he said, as if to convince himself. "I'll bet we do make it." He dressed from the head down. "Yes SIR." He went from slumped to determined in seconds, like a Jaguar shifting into high gear. I looked past Teddy's balls to his face, which was probably the right perspective. He wore the blank look of a man determined, once and for all, to set the VCR clock.

Teddy left. I watched gigantic shadows on three walls—mine, a spider's, one I didn't want to know about. I could lie down well enough, and stand in the middle, but the triangular proportions prevented pacing. Teddy's side of the bed remained warm well after he'd gone. I sometimes think woman's need for man is based solely on that: heat.

While flipping through cable TV stations, I contemplated the big Meet The Family gala. I worried that Teddy didn't have a real job, that he seemed in no hurry to move out of his parents' house. I worried about Phyllis, and all the Phyllises in all the three-month intervals in all the time I didn't know about.

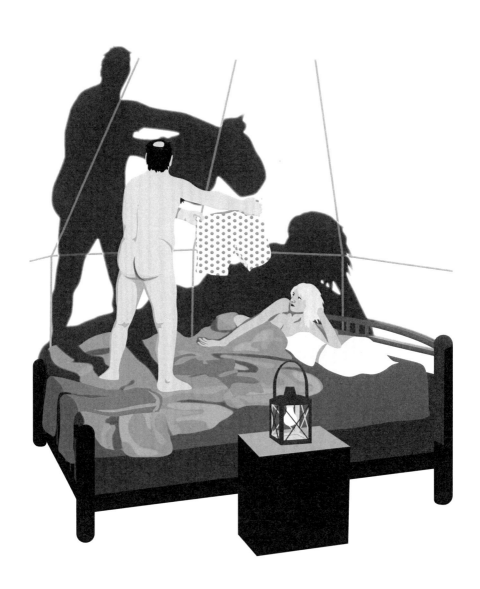

But work didn't mesh with Teddy's free spirit, and Mama's Boys were always the sweetest, and at least he'd told me about Phyllis. Right?

"Theodore tells me y'all met at church." Point of fact: we'd met in a little 50s juke joint that did a Wednesday night karaoke. Teddy serenaded me: Rodgers and Hammerstein's *People Will Say We're in Love*. He sent me a Sea Breeze. We talked. We kissed. He was in town visiting a cousin for a long weekend. I took sick days and acted as his tour guide. We were saying "I love you" before we even made it to the Arch.

"That's right," I said. Deceit seemed the wrong foot to get off on. Blasphemy, as well. But I couldn't very well overturn Teddy's lies, not in his own house.

As Mrs. Morganfield and the other Morganfield women set platter after platter of food on the table, I realized this could be a diet that worked: Southern cooking. Everything seemed gooey or half-alive. Some of it seemed gooey *and* half-alive. I watched Mr. Morganfield crumble corn bread into a glass of buttermilk, took fright when the science experiment slid down his Adam's apple in a series of gulps. He said "Damn!!!" and ran his tongue over his upper lip, like a "Got Goo?" commercial. Brussels sprouts, which looked like pterodactyl eggs about to hatch, made the rounds. Steaming okra was right behind. Yams. I tentatively placed a pinkish shellfish onto my plate, and when I looked away and looked back I swear it was on the other side of my turkey leg.

I spooned the tiniest, just-to-be-polite portions onto my plate. I hoped against hope the mashed potatoes and gravy were hidden somewhere beyond that mound of grits.

How can I explain okra? You know that weed that keeps sprouting in your backyard? Warm it up and throw a little salt on it. And yams? They're bright orange and smell like something you're rushing out to the garbage (Coming Through!!!).

I rope-a-dope-doped my dinner, mixed it around the plate with the fork, took little bites with big swigs of water, mixed some more, little bite, big water, little bite. In between, I fielded questions that came at me like bullets. "I hear from my son you're in the hospitality industry?" "Is that a good university, Washington University?" "Winters in Missoura must get mighty cold, not like the South."

It was hard to make eye contact with a bunch of strangers you wanted to like you when you were focused on choking down the third-to-last forkful of okra. I pretended each bite came from the specially prepared Claire plate Mom made me every Christmas in recognition of my "fussy eater" status. Yam became cranberry, okra turned into macaroni and cheese, corn bread transformed itself into a golden biscuit. Finally, I could see the bottom of my plate.

"Shou-ga? Would you like more yam?" Mrs. Morganfield asked.

The honest answer was: God no! But in that brief, jittery time when a polite, firm refusal should have tactfully tumbled from my mouth, I noticed Teddy looking at me in a way I thought might be judgmental. I said, "Yes, please," and then it was a yam convention on my plate. I gave myself a silent pep talk. Loaded up on white wine. Prayed. Loaded up on water. Took a breath.

I swallowed a big bite, washed it with water, washed it with white wine, held a napkin to my mouth to hide potential gagging. My eyes watered.

We went on like this a while—bite, white wine, water, napkin, repeat—before the meal mercifully ended. Us women cleaned supper dishes. The men sat around. I watched Teddy, unaware, through the doorway. Teddy. What did I really know about him? I was trying to remember. He had great hair. A nice smile. He was gentle and he treated people decently. I was like one of those savants that could make a new word from any existing word. Give me a man, any man, and I could make him a suitable lifelong partner.

As I twirled the cloth around a water glass, my attention shifted from Teddy to the uncles. They were all bald and fat and jolly. I looked back to Teddy: he already had the makings of a beer belly, and I'd lay odds he slapped backs. But it wasn't fair to gaze into the bald, fat uncle crystal ball. Was it?

Mrs. Morganfield said, "Shou-ga?" I'd only been in the family a day, but I already knew what followed would cause me some slight imposition.

"Shou-ga…" Mrs. Morganfield's voice jabbed me. "Why don't you start us off with *Go Tell It on the Mountain*?"

Singing, to me, is like, I don't know, answering the door naked. It's embarrassing. There's nothing to be gained by it. It's easily avoidable. My voice, which in my head precisely matches a familiar tune, actually matches a catfight in a closed aluminum garbage can.

Again, though: I was in their house. I cleared my throat. Aunt Somebody Or Other tinkled the piano. I sang, "Go, tell it, on the mount-Ain, Over the hills and ev-er-Y-where-Ere…" Aunt Somebody Or Other stopped. Aunt Somebody Else said, "Oh, dear."

The Morganfields ran a specialty music shop that sold old records, and rare sheet music, and memorabilia. They called it Way The Hell Off Broadway. Teddy worked there part-time and had aspirations to go full-time when business justified it.

Mrs. Morganfield intervened. "Dear," she said, "I do believe you're coming down with something."

That much was true. Teddy, nestled between several fat uncles on the sofa, spoke up. "Claire, you save that voice now," he said. "I've got an announcement to make later, and I do believe a round of toasts will follow."

The fat uncles and the fat Mr. Morganfield, along with the aunts and Mrs. Morganfield and a near-death grandmother, looked significantly at Theodore. Well, the grandmother's face was stuck that way. But the others: they *knew* something.

I massaged my throat. Christmas tunes followed Gospel tunes. Show tunes followed Christmas tunes. Even the kids—all Teddy's nieces and nephews—sang like little birds. A procession of anecdotes ensued: buying your first Ethel Merman record, seeing Barbara Streisand live. They recited lines from 30s and 40s Hollywood musicals. There were friendly arguments. ("I don't care if Jim Nabors *is* queer…") Through it all, I sat there with a stupid smile that said, "My throat."

I sank into my thoughts as Cole Porter and Andrew Lloyd Weber numbers swirled about the room. Did Teddy mean to pop the question? I'd relentlessly anticipated this moment. In the proposal of my imagination, the world turned fuzzy and my body turned warm and an orchestra swelled. A giddy chinking of champagne glasses sealed the deal. It wasn't like that now. No fuzziness, no warmth. No orchestra, unless you counted the Show Tune Carnival. No champagne.

One of Teddy's nephews sidled up to me. He'd thrashed his way from one side of the room to the other, knocking over nuts, cheese trays, and cousins on the way. I whispered, "Hello there, what's your name?"

He countered, "Who are you?"

"I'm your Uncle Teddy's friend Claire."

We held this interview in a far corner of the music room. He was maybe four years old.

"What are you doing here?" he persisted.

Excellent question. I tousled his hair, grinned at him and said, "I'm here to share the Christmas celebration..."

He whirled around and smacked a little girl who'd wandered into his path. I twisted him, by the shoulders, to face me. "Bad boy," I said. "You say you're sorry to her."

He stared deep into my eyes. He said, "You make me sad."

"Shou-ga..." The word had become a bluegrass bale to the side of my head. I pretended I hadn't heard.

Teddy, who'd left me alone to my own wiles, suddenly joined me on the couch. He snuggled close. Grabbed my hand and caressed my neck. He looked googly-eyed into my face and said, "Whatcha doing, sitting on the couch?"

I noticed, for the first time, that Teddy was always asking what you were doing when it was perfectly obvious what you were doing. If he saw you drying dishes, he'd say, "Whatcha doing, drying dishes?" If you were watching TV, he'd say, "Whatcha doing, watching TV?" If he saw you eating a taco, he'd say, "Whatcha doing, eating a taco?"

Teddy nuzzled me, all affectionate. It was the Coors. He said, "I always get this way around the holidays. I shouldn't drink so much." He crumpled the can in his hand. He went on, "The first step to admitting you have a problem is to admit you have a problem."

Mrs. Morganfield stepped closer. "Shou-ga. Our tradition, every

Christmas Eve, is we go a-caroling through the neighborhood. We prepare the hot chocolate—some of the a-dults prefer something stronger. Would you do us the honor of leading our little family procession?"

Why would I, the tin-eared stranger from St. Louis, be asked to host The Osmond Family Christmas? Mrs. Morganfield handed me a torch as we lined up outside the house.

"It's a job in itself managing the flame," Aunt First I'd Noticed Her said. "Don't mind about singing along."

Teddy, who'd disappeared, caught up with us halfway down the block. He fell in line behind me. "Whatcha doing, carrying the torch?" he asked.

I turned. The torchlight caught Teddy's sly face a certain way—a shit-eating grin, if ever I saw one. He winked at some fat uncle. They passed a flask around, tottering the whole time—*something stronger* apparently meant million-proof grain alcohol. "Yes sir," Teddy said. "Better warm up the video camera—we don't want to miss Claire's face when she opens up her gift."

The thing was, I didn't know what I would say, what I would do. I so wanted to be married. I dreaded the prospect of hunting down another potential life partner. There was so much preliminary blah blah blah you couldn't skip. Then if you guessed wrong, and so far I'd only guessed wrong, you were back at Square One. How was I ever going to get a baby blue Ford Explorer with She's The Boss vanity plates from Square One?

We were singing now. Or, *they* were singing—the ban was still in effect for me. We strolled up sidewalks en masse—*Silent Night, Away in a Manger, Little Town of Bethlehem.* Neighbors popped onto porches. Tiny faces huddled against big legs. Christmas trees glowed at us from living room windows. The crisp air was 20 degrees warmer than in St. Louis, where about now it would be freezing cold and possibly snowing. I smiled, my face awash in yellow torchlight. You could see everybody was thinking, "Who's *that*?" One man actually said it.

"This is Teddy's special friend, Claire," Mr. Morganfield said.

Special—that confirmed it. Back at the Morganfield place, I was installed for the night in a comfortable, elegant room. Comfortable and elegant—but not mine. Every Christmas Eve, me and my sister Cassie slept in our old room together, even though we both lived within ten miles of our parental home. I wanted badly to call. I wanted to hear Cassie say, as she would after peeking out the front room window, "Snow!!!!" But it might seem rude to make long-distance calls on the Morganfield phone.

I pulled the quilt up to my chin. I thought about being married, about being married to Teddy. I vacillated between No Way and I'll Do It. My nerves were wrecked. I was having an awful time. I missed my family. Teddy, in the light of day, had little chinks and bruises, water stains, big gaping cracks. Despite all this, I'll Do It presented a formidable case. Finding a husband exhausted all my energy. My life would remain angst-ridden, shallow and incomplete until I'd married. *No* meant more flirting in bars, more set-up dates, more tussles with Should I Call Him or Wait For Him To Call Me? *Yes* meant sitting on the local library board, china, struggles with Wallpaper or Paint?

Teddy might, after all, improve. Things weren't perfect but couldn't I look at it as a starting point?

As I burrowed my face into the Morganfield-scented pillow, I heard the door creak open, creak closed. Teddy's whispered, slurred voice said, "Whatcha doing, Claire, sleeping?"

"Shou-ga…"

I leaped from dream state to the stark, waking reality of Mrs. Morganfield's over-made face peering down at me. I panicked, briefly, but Teddy was long gone. Pink eyeliner that went from eyelashes clear to forehead blinded me like first light.

"Yes, Mrs. Morganfield."

"Y'all better get moving; we leave for Church in less than one hour."

Church. I was a Unitarian and Teddy's family devout Catholics. The faux pas danger level couldn't have been higher.

We traveled caravan-style to the church. I quizzed Teddy, en route, about mass: when did I stand up? When did I kneel? Any rituals or prayers I needed to cram for? He assured me it was a game of follow-the-leader.

The subtext to our conversation, though, was: impending proposal. His good humor, his patience, that church tie, all said EARNEST SUITOR.

In all my relationships leading up to this point, I'd begged for this very situation. It was such a short leap from Saying I Do to Hosting A Couples Costume Party. Now, though: I didn't know how to interpret my own quivering.

Church went okay until Communion. The entire congregation filed out of their pews. I took my place in line. I carefully observed the way some people took the wafer on their tongue, the way other people took it in their cupped hands. I did the cupped hands. I walked, slowly, somberly, back toward our section. I popped the wafer into my mouth. What I didn't count on…the wafer was so dry.

I sputtered and gagged, bowed down my head and held in the vomit. Teddy whispered, "Whatcha doing, Claire, gagging on the Communion wafer?"

Aunt Somebody Else said, "I told you she's coming down with something."

"Shou-ga."

The moment approached. I still didn't have an answer. I tried to mentally rally myself to the cause. I could more plainly hear myself saying, "Oh Teddy…Teddy, yes," than, "I hate to say this in front of the whole family…"

"Yes, Mrs. Morganfield."

"Do me a big old favor and pass out the presents. Just so you know, we get the little ones going first, and then each a-dult gets one present in turn."

I lowered myself to the floor. All the little nieces and nephews crunched toward me. The "sitting room" in which we gathered held an Old World charm. The tree lights and candles cast poignant slivers of light. The soothing smell of blended pine needles, eggnog and potpourri floated about the house. Everybody seemed snuggly content. Well, not me. I was sweating like some unidentifiable farm animal we'd eaten for Christmas dinner.

I didn't remember the names of the fat uncles, or the aunts, much less the nieces and nephews. Meaning, I had to bluff. I picked up a present. "Trevor," I called out. I scanned the relatives, as if of course I knew little Trevi but couldn't readily spot him among a crowd of 14.

Trevor charged the present, took it from my hand, ran off with it. "Timmy?" Again, I screwed a "Now where did I last see that cuddly little Timmy?" look on my face. One of the fat uncles bellowed from the back, "Right here."

"Right," I said. The tag should have read, "Enormous, Jolly, Bald Uncle Timmy With The Hee-Haw Laugh." I handed him his present. "Hold this until I get all the little ones a box."

I read through more tags, trying to guess which were children, which were adults. I also scouted for my own name. Would it be a box-in-a-box-in-a-box situation, with the ring box finally staring out at me?

"Bridget?" The You Make Me Sad kid sat to my right. He peered up at me. He accused, "You don't know our names." I patted his head— "cute kid."

"Bridget's home with a bad flu," Mrs. Morganfield said.

"What's my name?" You Make Me Sad asked.

I got through it. The kids grabbed presents and scampered off to various corners, like wild animals with their share of the carrion. The adults—basically, everybody gave everybody else Liza Minnelli CDs. There we were, at the end. I became a little embarrassed about my gift to Teddy, which in just a few minutes would seem so very insufficient. I said, red-faced, "I've got something for Teddy."

He opened my gift like you'd open a can of chewing tobacco. He used a hunting knife from his pocket to punch a hole, then tore back the paper with his claws. "Sweater," he said. He cocked a loaded finger at me and shot.

Then: Teddy stood up. "We're not quite through, y'all," he said. Mine, I could see it coming, was going to be dramatic. He hustled into the back bedroom. I stood there in the middle of all the Morganfields. They looked at me. I looked at them. They pretended not to know what was next. I pretended not to know what was next. They knew. I knew.

"Okay, okay." Teddy returned with a wrapped present...*not* the size of a ring. It looked, rather, like an oversized tennis racket. That, I guessed immediately, was part of the gag.

"I've got an announcement," Teddy declared. The room fell silent, except for the kids, who were playing with their new toys. "I want to say, thanks to Claire for coming to Kentucky for Christmas, we're glad to have her."

"Everybody raise your cans," a fat uncle bellowed. Beer cans, champagne glasses: it was all the same. The family stood poised. "To Claire's first Morganfield family Christmas," he said.

After a few swigs, a few hear hears, Teddy turned to me. He handed me the present. "Claire, Merry Christmas. Open her up."

It probably *was* a tennis racket. But then at the bottom of the can of balls, there would be the ring. I stalled, trying to figure out my reaction, my response. I tried to figure out the rest of my life. To be honest, I felt a little like I'd hit the star as well, or more I'd realized the prize was so incidental I should never have played the game in the first place. Yet—*what was wrong with me?*—I couldn't pass up this chance.

I was this close to adopting my own sea lion named Paddy from the zoo. Ever so close to the perfect brownie recipe. A hair away from Bridge Night with the Fontanas.

I opened the present. Snow…shoes. I lifted the snowshoes, tried to shake loose the diamond engagement ring.

"Snowshoes," Teddy said. He smiled a Presidential smile, from one end of the room to the other.

That was the gift. Not an engagement ring. Not Teddy on his knees asking me to spend the rest of my life with him and his Glee Club family.

"Yes, sir," Teddy said. "Snowshoes. Not just any old snowshoes, either. These are absolute top-of-the-line. You'd crap if you knew what I paid."

Rather, a pair of high-end snowshoes. Tears welled up in my eyes. I tried to thank Teddy but struggled to speak.

"Whatcha doing, crying?" he asked.

It was the best gift I'd ever gotten.

"Aren't you just flabbergasted?" Teddy asked. "Aunt Emily said twasn't romantic enough, but the heck with romantic, these are doggone good snowshoes."

I jumped up and hugged Teddy. We kissed. It was our third-to-last kiss. Teddy raised his hands to shush the crowd. He raised his beer can. "A toast," he said, "to some good snowshoeing weather back in Missoura."

Aunt Forgot Her Name Already hummed. Aunt You Can Take Off The Apron Now hummed lower. Some Morganfields took the lead, some fell to the harmony. There were Morganfields singing bass, Morganfields singing alto. I joined in the chorus—loud, horribly off key—but I didn't care. Soon, I'd be in transport from Cave City back to St. Louis. Next year, there'd be no mistakes: I'd be home for Christmas.

Tiny Flakes of Bone

On the phone, we agreed this wasn't about gambling. It was about two bachelors doing a nice bachelor Christmas. But there was Buddy Brandon, all lit up under the blinking "Jackpot, Jackpot, Jackpot" sign. He pulled the slot machine lever and yelled, "You *Shit*," "You *Little* Shit." He pulled again: "You Little *Fucking* Shit!" The lovely flight attendant smiled at me, as if to say, "Welcome to Las Vegas." Buddy seemed to move in jerks, like somebody's half-drunk, discoing dad. Ch-ching, ch-ching, ch-chings drowned out the coming-and-going plane sounds.

   "We'll go to Liberace's house," he'd said.

"The clown factory," I'd added.

"Red Rock Canyon."

   It was early afternoon Christmas Eve. Back in Detroit, Christmas SHOUTED at you—reindeer and elves and garland and Wise Men. From the window of my stalled plane, snowflakes swirled about, appearing to float, float, float, and never land.

Here, Christmas whispered—the odd cardboard Santa or red felt hat. Fine with me. A Christmas that looked like Christmas would only remind me of home, and a trail of Christmases that led here.

I crept behind Buddy, and watched over his right shoulder through three losing pulls. His big left hand dipped for quarters. His big right hand engulfed an orange-and-yellow asthma spray can and the lever. He said, without turning around, "If your piece-of-shit plane gets here on schedule I'm up a hundred and a half." He puffed from his asthma spray can without breaking rhythm. Pull, puff, pull.

"Ride up to Hoover Dam!"

"Eat dinner up on the Stratosphere."

Buddy went six-five, and his weight yo-yoed between two and a quarter and, say, three even. Egyptian ancestors somewhere on his mom's side gave him a dark, hairy complexion. By five o'clock his shadow amounted to a beard.

"An hour twelve minutes late," I said.

"Instead of making a buck and a half I dumped a quarter." He puffed again. "I should sue fucking American Airlines."

Buddy was my oldest friend, going back to when we worked at Ford. We were both people who'd heard, "You really need to stop gambling." Depending on your definition of "stop," neither of us had done too well.

I sat down next to Buddy. I had that old leaf-in-the-wind feeling, and I wondered if I truly had the self-control to not gamble. I wondered if I really wanted that. I wondered—I was 52, after all—if I'd long passed that point at which recovery held any meaning. Was I already who I was going to be?

We were 15 minutes between landing and baggage claim. Fifteen minutes doesn't sound like much, but consider how long it takes to drop a quarter into the slot, pull the lever, and wait for the fruit to stop. You can do a whole lot of good or a whole lot of damage in 15 minutes. Buddy lost another 25: "You *Shit*!" "You *Little* Shit!!" "You Little *Fucking* Shit!!!" My machine paid out on my first three pulls, and I made 50.

"Sit by the pool," he'd insisted.

"Drive past Charo's place."

After we claimed my bags, Buddy said, "First thing, right off, we go food shopping."

It was a sunny, 60-something degree afternoon. We had windows down and t-tops off. Suntanned drivers peered through sunglasses at the shimmering graphite road; pop and rap and country and jazz bass lines pulsated from car stereos; ant-like people moved in and out of casino parking lots. I fidgeted in my seat. The feeling I got here was as close as I ever got to recapturing that childhood feeling of counting down the days, minutes and seconds until my release from a confined, paralytic classroom into a sprawling, high-octane playground. The possibilities, in spite of everything, never ceased to beckon.

We crossed Las Vegas Boulevard, and Buddy said, "That's what's known as The Strip. Basically, it's casinos and hotels as far as the eye can see. You go north, that's downtown." I'd been to Las Vegas plenty, I'd stayed with Buddy plenty, but every time he acted like it was my first time. Buddy asked about Tanya. He knew some of the story but not all. I'd moved out and more and more it had the feel of permanent relocation. She was my second wife. "We fight once a week whether we need to or not," I said. I added, "We're still working on it."

Buddy said, "I've always contended she was a nut case."

Buddy was right, but I was no blue ribbon myself. The kids, some Tanya's, some Marianne's, were grown up and scattered around the country. They were only vaguely interested in our split up.

Buddy pulled up to his apartment complex gate. He waved to the security guard. He inched into the parking lot, and then idled near the pool. "See that?" he asked.

"The pool?"

"The high dive. I installed that, more or less. Nice, huh?"

The pool was empty, and a withered old lady lay sunning on the high dive board. "Fine," I said. Buddy indicated one second with his index finger, jumped out of the car, disappeared around the bend, and returned in two minutes. He stuffed what looked like parlay cards in his front shirt pocket.

Buddy worked building maintenance in exchange for free rent and a small salary. Mostly, he changed locks. It was a low-end complex, but nice enough. Transients and struggling families lived there. If a tenant missed a rent payment, Buddy went in and changed the lock. He changed six, seven locks a day. There were three hundred units in this complex, plus the pool, plus a little weight room. Lots of times, the families never came back to claim their shit. Buddy put everything off to the side—"it's there for them if they want it, within a certain time frame"—and after a while transferred it to his own apartment.

Buddy kept promising to make use of these things. He had water skis for when he learned to water ski, and a bunch of Sega game cartridges for when he got a Sega, and an aviator suit for when he learned to pilot his own plane, and a collection of Spanish novels on tape for when he learned to speak Spanish.

Buddy hit the gas. "Did you get lunch on the plane?" he asked.

Albertson's was near Buddy's apartment complex, which was west of The Strip. "Trail mix and a Coke."

"Never go grocery shopping hungry," he said.

He wheeled the car sharply down Flamingo, over The Strip again to Paradise, back on Desert Inn Road, and parked it in a lot behind the Desert Inn Hotel. "Thing about Vegas, they got buffets'll knock your socks off. It's part of the strategy to get tourists to gamble more: cheap food, free liquor. The hotels, they write off the food. But if you play it right, do it the smart way, it's just eating cheap." In a matter of minutes we were at a white table-clothed table with a view of what passed for the tropics. There was a lagoon-shaped swimming pool, lush gardens, and palm trees.

Buddy grabbed two sheets of paper and two pencils from between the salt and pepper shakers, in the place you'd expect napkins or maybe *How Was The Service?* cards. He handed me a set. "They play keno one game after another. Keno is like bingo, only better. You can circle two numbers, three numbers, ten, twenty. Circle as many as you want. The more you pick right, the bigger the payout. A girl comes around, takes your numbers, brings your winnings if you win. You can play anywheres from a dollar up."

"I know how to play Keno, Buddy."

We circled numbers. The Keno girl came around as if summoned by telepathy. Buddy and I handed her our cards and cash, then watched her walk away. She wore heels, nylons and a garter. Her tight, sparkly outfit was cut low in front and short short in the back. "Man, I forget...this is some town," I said.

"And they have to be nice to you, it's how they get tips," Buddy said. "The board's over there if you want to follow." He pointed behind me at an electronic board with numbers flashing on and off every 30 seconds.

At Ford, they called me Big Fred, or just Big. I wasn't as big as Buddy but we were shopping off the same rack. An endless spread greeted us. I started small—crab cakes, potato soup, salad—and the Keno Girl swooped by to check our old cards and take new ones to the cashier.

"You *Shit*! Know who's in town?" Buddy asked. "That Dice Man funny man. You *Little* Shit!! Guy that does that hard-ass comedy routine. You Little *Fucking* Shit!!!"

I worked my way up to turkey and gravy with mashed potatoes, and our girl wiggled past to change cards again. I did a second main course of chicken in red sauce and some cheesy potatoes, and by now me and the Keno Girl were old friends. She showed up while I nibbled on all the stuff I couldn't pronounce—Coq au Vin and a "tournedo" of beef. Again during brownies and ice cream, and again while Buddy and I sat with our buttons popped. All the while, white numbers flashed on the black board. I won a couple free cards—flash, flash, and off one of those I hit on four numbers—flash, flash, flash, flash. I made enough to cover my losses, the meal, and a little more. Buddy played every card for big money, but— YOU LITTLE *FUCKING* SHIT!!!—never won.

"See Buddy Hackett."

"How about Phyllis Diller?"

He was right, the buffet was dirt-cheap. But this was definitely a case of Desert Inn 1, Buddy Nothing.

"Now," Buddy said as we headed back to the car. "We shop with our heads not our stomachs." He pointed at his greasy, tangled, kinky hair.

Before we met up with cereal or ketchup or lunchmeat, we ran into a bank of slot machines. "Oh, yeah, Big," Buddy bragged. "We got gambling in the grocery stores. We got gambling in the movie theaters, the drug stores. We even got gambling in the 7-11s."

Buddy lost a couple bucks—You *Shit*!!—but I hit three cherries on three quarters—ring, ring, ring, SPISSSH—and connected for double bars—cah-ching, cah-ching, ca-ching—then triple bars—SPISSSH. I netted up near a hundred and a half. "Let's stop right here, Buddy. Let's do the grocery shopping, and do it right."

This was how it was supposed to work: winning. We bought the best-cut pot roast, "gourmet" instant mashed potatoes, fresh-baked pumpkin pie. We loaded the grocery cart: this and that, Doritos, cheese whiz, crackers. We bought good beer—*eight-dollar-a-six* beer. Egg nog. Little chocolate reindeers—"candies," it said on the box. We skimped on nothing. If it was a choice between store brand toilet paper and Charmin's, we went with Charmin's. Our asses were going to be treated right this Christmas.

We checked out.

Buddy rearranged my luggage, as well as a big, sealed box, to make room in the trunk for the groceries. We were off for his apartment.

"You gotta take into account the three-hour time swing," Buddy said as he merged with traffic. "One o'clock games wind up being ten o'clock games. Four o'clock games go off at one. You're not going to want to get up that early to make bets. Let's get our plays down now; just-for-fun bets. Besides, you gotta see the Rio's Christmas tree: it's the biggest Christmas tree in the...I think in the world."

Buddy's Buick needed a new muffler and brakes and tires. But it was clean and the radio worked and every time his t-tops got stolen he replaced them right away. Palm trees divided Flamingo Boulevard. Dusky mountains rose up to the north, south and east. Skyscraper hotels rose up to the west. White peaks capped the mountains.

I thought I should say something about Buddy's latest ex-wife, but I knew it would be unpleasant, and, really, what was there to say? Sadie had run off with a Circus Circus dealer, along with Buddy's modest savings account, just four months before. Gambling losses, tied together with general misfortune, kept him perpetually on the edge of solvency. First wife—Buddy was just a kid then—died, insuranceless, of breast cancer, which was Bankruptcy Number One. Second wife bought it in a car crash, and Buddy insisted on top-shelf funeral arrangements, which wiped him out again. Sadie wiped him out a third time.

Buddy got giddy all over again every time he found out he could keep the car and a thousand bucks worth of furniture. I should mention they called him Bad Luck Buddy Brandon down at the Ford plant. Nicest guy you'd ever want to meet. Kind of guy, he'd cut his right arm off for a friend—if it weren't in hock.

"That there white, that's snow," Buddy said, pointing. "I shit you not, Big. You can lay by the pool down here in the valley, go up to the mountains and SKI." Buddy lived for this tour-guide shit, but you had to take everything he said with a grain of salt. What he didn't know, he made up.

He eased the car into the Rio parking lot. "The Rio, it's owned by Steve Wynn. I think Steve Wynn owns it, owns half this town in any event, and he's only like 40 years old. What people don't talk about, this town makes people, too. Everybody's quick with a story about Las Vegas ruining somebody, so let's be fair."

I underestimated how much warmer it'd be in Vegas than Detroit. I went into Buddy's trunk, moved that cardboard box again, and had Buddy shield me as I changed. I traded long for short sleeves, jeans for shorts, boots for sandals. I felt looser.

We walked across the warm blacktop toward the glittering red Rio sign. A red slash, kind of like lipstick on a mirror, underlined the name. We stood beneath the mammoth Christmas tree near the entrance. It went almost as high as the casino roof. There was no breeze, only sun. Buddy said, "That's the big Christmas tree."

"I see that," I said.

We went inside and made bets. Innocent, low stakes bets. Purely entertainment, I told myself. Not crazy, taking-out-third-mortgages kinds of bets. We each picked a couple games then filled out a parlay card together. Buddy said, "One quick drink to toast your arrival."

We sat at the bar, and you can't actually sit at the bar without playing video poker. I mean, they won't let you. Bar seats are reserved for gamblers.

"To a friendship which outlasted five marriages."

He was already counting Tanya. We played roll after roll of quarters. The cards blipped on the screen, and we poked at the buttons—hold, deal, play credits—while talking about old times and our Christmas Day plans.

"I got a book," Buddy said, "will tell us what's open on the holidays—You *Shit*!—and what's not. Liberace's House, I gotta guess that'd be open—You *Little* Shit! It's got all his getups in there. You should see some of them: they got so much gold on them—You Little *Fucking* Shit!!!—I bet they weigh like 200 pounds."

We both had cold machines. But then right at the end I hit four-of-a-kind—blip, blip, blip, BLIP—and netted up. We cashed out. My coins clink, clink, clinked into the metal tray like a beautiful rainfall. For Buddy, it was another dry desert day.

Buddy insisted we make one more quick trip. "They got this bowl game contest at the Stardust," Buddy said. "With the Blue-Gray Game going on tomorrow—I just remembered—I gotta turn in my picks tonight. I wish I remembered earlier, that's back the way we came." The fiery orange sun dropped behind the hills, and at the same time red and yellow and orange and blue neon flickered on all down The Strip.

"Okay," I said. Jet lag dragged me down a bit. I thought about a nap, and Buddy's pool, and those eight-dollar-a-six beers.

"The Houdini Museum."

"They got a chocolate factory does tours, free of charge."

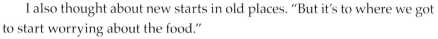

I also thought about new starts in old places. "But it's to where we got to start worrying about the food."

"Did you notice I didn't buy no ice cream?"

"I guess so."

"That was deliberate."

"The pot roast?"

"That had to thaw anyway."

The sky turned from light to dark blue. To the west, the Stratosphere needle of the old Landmark, through some optical illusion, appeared taller than the surrounding mountains. Buddy drove down Industrial Boulevard, and I didn't know the exact geography but by now I could tell we'd been crossing and recrossing The Strip. It was like a huge magnet that kept drawing us back. He parked in the Stardust lot. A sign shaped like a lopsided heart and filled with neon stars shot straight up maybe 200 feet into the air. "You always come in the back side and leave the car," Buddy said. "The locals know better than to try and drive The Strip."

Buddy prided himself on being local. You could hardly wrangle out of him that he grew up just the other side of Gratiot Avenue, worked his grandfather's poultry stand at the Eastern Market, went to Cass Tech, took early retirement from Ford. He tried to pass himself off as a semi-professional gambler, and only if you prodded would he mention the maintenance job.

Buddy pulled those cards from his front shirt pocket. He grabbed a pencil nub from the sports window. He examined the betting board. Teams and score totals blipped and changed. The wall stretched from one end of the room to the other—college football, pro football, college basketball, pro basketball, hockey, future bets, proposition bets, money-line bets, the flats, the buggies.

We were standing there, necks craned, watching orange and green and red numbers change as bets got placed and scores shifted. Different games and races played on each of a hundred TV sets.

"Pet the Siegfried & Roy white tigers!!"

Gamblers cheered their games or looked up at the board like me and Buddy. At the tables, there were individual TV sets.

"What do you think of West Virginia?" Buddy asked.

Once you give up gambling, you realize, "Who the fuck knows?" But when you're in the middle of it, you've got an opinion about every school that could afford a football and some shoulder pads. Somebody asked you how do you like Creighton or how do you like Grambling or how do you like Drake, you launched into a detailed explanation—based mostly on the fact that the team had screwed you at some point—about what would happen and why, right down to the final score. I gave Buddy my thoughts and then like any gambler he ignored what I said and did what he was going to do before he asked me.

Buddy turned in his card. On the way out, he stopped at a roulette table. "Let's watch one minute," he said. The ball rolled, rolled, rattled, rattled, settled on six. "Six, Al Kaline's number," Buddy said. He reached into his pocket. Bought fifty dollars worth of chips. "I got a system," he said. "If the first number comes up is one of the Tigers' all-time starting eight, it's a play. You put a chip on each of the seven remaining starters."

"This is silly-ass shit, Buddy," I said.

"You repeat until the other seven come up, or until the wheel goes three in a row without a Tigers all-star. Double up if a starting pitcher comes up. I swear to God, it works eight, nine times out of ten."

We grew up three blocks from each other and never knew it until Ford. I didn't have to ask who the eight all-stars were. We first hit it off talking about going to The Stick as kids. Buddy scattered chips on seven numbers. Nothing. He put chips on the same seven numbers. Twenty-five, Norm Cash, came up. "Champion system," Buddy said.

His eyes were glued to the red and black and green and gold roulette wheel; our conversation was done. I roamed over to the five-dollar blackjack table. I was silently grateful, more than grateful, to ride out my lucky streak. I felt my arms spreading for the long, thrilling, sense-defying leap. I hit blackjacks on two of my first four hands. I played two more hands and won on dealer busts. Every once in a while, through chirping and clinking and screeching, I heard, "You *Shit*! You *Little* Shit!! You Little *Fucking* Shit!!!"

I don't know how long he'd been there, but Buddy was standing over my shoulder puffing his asthma spray. I played another hand and won. Chips were piling up in front of me. I looked at Buddy like, "Well?" and he shook his head like, "No good." The dealer clapped her hands—a magician, nothing up her sleeve—to indicate she'd finished her shift. The new dealer shuffled two shoes together. Buddy suggested he hold onto half my winnings so's to keep me from blowing all the profits. We'd done this for each other before on the theory you always give it all back but if you don't have it to give back you'll walk away a winner. I agreed, and Buddy took a pile of my chips. He left.

The second dealer was as good to me as the first, and Buddy's voice— "You *Little* Shit!!!"—foreshadowed Buddy's appearances, to confiscate my winnings. Each time I gave him the look like, "Well?" and each time he shook his head, like, "Losing my dick."

It'd been a while since I'd seen Buddy. Though I stood stationary, I felt as though I were twirling, spinning, double tucking. There's a premonition you get sometimes when you're in the casino, a premonition, "You better go find your friend." I had that feeling now. I colored up—traded small for big chips—and took a lap around the casino. Buddy was nowhere to be found.

I wandered from one casino to another, and back again, traveling a network of skyways and indoor cannels and escalators and elevators. Buddy might be here, he might be next door, he might be across the street. Who knew? All the while, amazing and bright things, like volcanoes erupting, happened. I told myself one of us needed to stay put, and this roulette table would be my anchor.

A Ray Charles impersonator sang in the lounge. I didn't even know which lounge, though judging by the cocktail waitress I figured I was in Treasure Island.

For about a half-hour a nutty woman with a purple scarf bet the number one on every spin. She played one through *Georgia on My Mind*, she played one through *What'd I Say*, she played one through *Hit the Road Jack*.

Never came up. Finally, she busted out and left the table. I put a pile of chips on the one, another pile on the red, a third pile on odd, another pile on first third. Bingo: it came up one.

I asked the dealer to hold my spot, and shot off to the bathroom. When I came back, Buddy was standing there with a big grin. I felt a great sense of relief. One, there he was. Two, I figured the smile meant his own luck had turned. But no: while I was pissing *I'd* won a big pile. In my rush to get to the john, I'd forgotten to take my chips off the table, in which event the dealer always lets the original wager ride. It came up one again.

"This is a sign. Let's go now, Buddy," I said. I didn't mean it. I'd lost all track of everything, everything except an overwhelming desire to come out right, just this once.

Time's a mystery in the casinos. There aren't any clocks or windows, and pumped oxygen keeps you unnaturally energized. I felt juiced. It's like, you're minding your own business, and there's a fire engine, and you don't even realize you're chasing the fire engine—you never decided, here I go after the fire engine—but before you know it you're on the lawn watching the house burn down. Buddy probably picked that up in my voice.

"You're hot," he said. "You're fucking red hot." I was. I was hot. I was *red* hot. Buddy took some of my new winnings. He said something I could hardly make out, his lips out of sync with his words, then turned over his wrist and looked at the place where there would have been a watch if he had a watch. "Let's call it an hour."

Buddy took a puff of his asthma spray, and I watched his big Egyptian frame bowl through the crowd. His weight shifted all the way from one side to the other, like how you'd move an oven to sweep behind it. I played some more. Won a little, won a little more, won a lot.

"They got a Neon Museum I'd like to see."

I couldn't tell anymore if it was day or night, yesterday or tomorrow, but I suspected it was nearing Christmas morning.

Crowds of people flooded the streets, and traffic backed up for miles in either direction. It felt more like a play about Christmas than Christmas itself. I was disoriented and couldn't say which way was which.

For the next I don't know how many hours, I gambled. I won at some carnival-like wheel game. "This here's more you got in safe keeping," Buddy said. I won at slots. "I'm keeping track." I won a horse race in Tokyo. "This goes toward the total.!!!!" The theory that one or the other would always be the voice of reason worked opposite with me and Buddy. If Buddy couldn't think of something insanely stupid on his own, I took personal responsibility for coming up with the insanely stupid thing.

"You ever think about playing a round of golf?"

It occurred to me—it was just a passing thought—that my chips were like those abandoned apartment items, that if I didn't come by to claim ownership in a reasonable time Buddy would transfer them to his own pile.

I wandered: cabs and shuttles, tunnels and back doors, escalators and elevators. Glittering dome ceilings and chandeliers, and ch-chinging slots, and cocktail waitresses in skimpy Pirate and Egyptian and Bunny outfits, and free drinks, free drinks, free drinks. Caesar's to the Mirage to the Luxor to downtown joints like the Golden Nugget and Fitzgerald's and Lady Luck. Big tips to cabbies and cocktail waitresses and dealers. Sing-alongs to Abba and David Cassidy and Barry Manilow.

The entire world spun and clanged and swished in time to my new life as a big-time winner.

I'd been promising myself when I saw Buddy again I'd be firm, tell him we had to go home, we had to go home NOW, but I no longer, in the slightest, wanted to go home. Piss on the nice bachelor Christmas.

When I next saw Buddy, he was standing in an outside pedestrian area. "This is called The Freemont Experience," Buddy narrated, as though we'd been touring the town together all along. "It uses something like a trillion watts of electricity—is that right, a trillion?, I think that's right—on an average weekend during the summer."

A black dome covered a narrow strip of sidewalks, smaller casinos on either side. I watched a bunch of neon reindeer trot along the roof, and then a jolly old neon Santa in a red neon sleigh. *Here Comes Santa Claus* accompanied the neon ride. I watched neon reindeer reflected in Buddy's ashen face, and thought I should ask about my chips. Instead, I stood there mesmerized, not able or willing to investigate further a moment when the universe seemed on my side.

The cards and numbers finally stopped going my way. I was punch drunk, and regular drunk, and emotionally drained. For once, I did the smart thing: I quit while I was ahead. True, I'd lost back my operating capital, but I still had my Buddy winnings. Only thing was, I didn't have Buddy. Christmas Eve had come and gone. We were well into Christmas Day. The crowd had thinned considerably, and now you couldn't tell the late night from the early morning addicts. Then, across the plush red carpeting of the Golden Nugget, somewhere beyond the cordoned high-stakes poker area, I spotted him. He stood poised by a slot machine. I could see he was pushing his upper weight limit now; too many buffets no doubt. His eyes were red, his shirt half tucked in, half tucked out. He'd grown a beard. One hand stayed buried in his fanny pouch, and the other stayed on the lever. He removed the asthma spray from the fanny pack, and puffed. Only it broke rhythm, no pull, just a long puff. As I got closer, I saw his lever hand go to an empty pouch hand, and then a cocktail waitress came by with a drink. He didn't tip her. As I got within hearing distance, I tuned my ear for Buddy's refrain—"You *Shit*," "You *Little* Shit," "You Little *Fucking* Shit." Nothing. That was when I knew: Buddy was out of money. The casinos only give free drinks to gamblers, and Buddy was pretending to gamble so he could get another free drink.

When I finally made it to Buddy, we stood there a beat. He said, his voice filled with shame and self-loathing, "Well, you can pretty well guess what happened."

"Tank's on full," Buddy said.

"I hope that's not the fucking silver lining," I said.

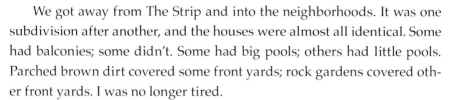

We got away from The Strip and into the neighborhoods. It was one subdivision after another, and the houses were almost all identical. Some had balconies; some didn't. Some had big pools; others had little pools. Parched brown dirt covered some front yards; rock gardens covered other front yards. I was no longer tired.

"You know who has lawns in Las Vegas?" Buddy asked.

"Who?" I said.

"Rich people, that's who. You got to remember, we get just about zilch rain out here, and it's fucking hot all the time. So it takes a minor fortune to be watering a lawn two, three times every day. They got Astro turf at my complex, which is great for the maintenance people."

I didn't say anything. I wanted him to...I don't know what I wanted. An apology wouldn't help. Promises were no good. My fault, Buddy's fault: none of it mattered. I just wanted to be mad. "You still want to go to Liberace's house?" he asked.

"I'm not exactly in a Liberace's house mood just at the moment."

"They got a whole wall of Liberace with all the famous people he knows."

"Let's put it this way," I said. "We can't afford Liberace's house."

The sun was up high over the mountains. Behind us, the tall buildings of The Strip painted a weaving single-file skyline. We zoomed past a Tom Jones billboard and Buddy said, "Tom Jones, he's a hero in this town." I didn't respond. "Wayne Newton too. You can hardly go a night without hearing *Danke Schoen*. You like *Danke Schoen*?"

"I don't know. I doubt it."

"Oh, how can you not like *Danke Schoen*?" He started singing it. "Danke Schoen, darling, Danke Schoen. Thanks for all the joy and pain...."

The farther we got from The Strip, the more it seemed like desert. Everything that wasn't a subdivision was a mall or a construction site. Buildings were being thrown up everywhere. Slanted clay roofs, adobe facades, off-white and peach paint. Saguaro cactuses in nearly every yard. The blueprints were so similar...you wouldn't want to try to find your house drunk.

"One thing you gotta see, then home," he said. "There's a street, they call this street Christmas Row. Everybody on the block goes balls out for Christmas."

I wasn't talking. Buddy kept doing his tour-guide shtick as we crawled down the block. There were lawn scenes, and fancy decorations, and trees. "Of course, you really want to see this at night to get in a proper Christmas spirit," Buddy said.

"Ho, ho, ho," I said.

We crept to the end of the street, which dead ended in a massive construction zone. The Earth looked like it does in Road Runner cartoons: packed red clay with wide cracks, an occasional soft brown weed straining through the surface. Backhoes and dumpsters and bulldozers were scattered about. A sign announced the coming of another subdivision.

Buddy stopped the car. "You see that?"

"The only thing I want to see is a bed," I said.

"That couch," Buddy said.

An orange couch, so close to the color of Earth as to seem camouflaged, sat in the middle of the construction site. It had a big dumpster off to one side, and a Porta Potty off to the other. Buddy eased the car to a curb spot, and got out. I wanted to see it too. My whole ambition in life, as regarded my wrecked finances, was to someday pass an abandoned couch without even slowing down. But I wasn't there yet. I watched from the car as Buddy plopped down. I heard him say, "Oh, my God." He got up and looked under the cushions, checked the springs. Buddy had gotten in the habit of confiscating abandoned objects first, asking questions later. I got out of the car. I could not think beyond the next few seconds, or perhaps I didn't want to know. I sat down. Until that very moment, I didn't think I could ever sleep again, but as soon as I sank into that big, cushy couch my body went limp. I closed my eyes. "Alls we need now is that pot roast," I said.

"That reminds me," he said. I felt the springs on Buddy's side ease, and the sun beat down on my body. It felt nice after the air-conditioned casinos. I nodded off for what must have been two minutes, and woke thinking I'd been asleep hours. Buddy set down the cardboard box that had been in his trunk. He set down a paper grocery bag. Blood from the pot roast had gotten all over everything. Buddy glanced at his shirt sleeve, then tugged it down to cover his club of a right hand. He wiped blood off a bottle before opening and handing me a warm beer, then wiped blood off a bag of chips before tearing it open with his teeth. He balanced the chips on the couch arm. He wiped blood off the salsa jar, twisted it open and set it next to the chips. He wiped blood off his own beer, opened it and took a big swig.

"Do you think the construction crew will be happy to find us out here?" I asked.

"They don't work on Christmas," Buddy said.

We sipped our warm beer. In a way we were about to execute our original plans: I had four more days in Vegas and we sure weren't going to be doing any more gambling. I loaded a chip with salsa and bit into it. Buddy knelt down on the red clay, his beer beside him. He unfolded the cardboard box flaps.

"I found these the day before you got here," he said.

"I just got here yesterday."

"Day before yesterday."

Buddy removed a plastic Grand Canyon snow dome, then a Pike's Peak one. He set them up on the opposite couch arm. "It's a collection. Hundreds of these little shake-em-up things. Trips they must of taken. Some of them are cheap, but there's some serious high-end ones, too. Those got stone bases."

He kept pulling out snow domes—Popeye, Alcatraz Swim Team, Alice In Wonderland—and setting them around the couch, on the back, off to the side, on the top of the dumpster, in front of the Porta Potty. "There's more beer," Buddy said.

"Give me one," I said.

We started on our second warm beers, and by now snow globes surrounded our little area. A wedding couple snow globe. Piccadilly Circus snow globe. An angel with the globe part for a belly. A snow globe advertising dandruff shampoo. Old Faithful snow globe. All the Christmas snow globes. Wild West snow scenes. State and sports team snow domes.

"Take a look at this," Buddy said. He shook up two kids on a teeter-totter, and set it down. Shook up a golfer, and set it down.

"Doesn't make sense," I said. "If it were snowing, he wouldn't be playing golf."

"That's not the point," he said. "What I'm showing you is the flakes. There's a book goes with them. Know what the book says they're made of?" He shook up a happy birthday cake.

I sipped the warm beer and looked across at all the idle construction equipment. I looked down Christmas Row. Buddy shook two snow globes at a time, then returned them to the ground.

"They're made of bone. Little bone shavings. Well, some of them are made of plastic, but others...bone. Tiny flakes of bone."

I didn't know what to say to that. I finished another beer, and Buddy got me a third. "You're not as cute as the other cocktail waitresses," I said.

We were laughing. There was snow coming down in all the little domes.

"I'm surprised the back hoe doesn't come with a craps table," he said. "Or that the bulldozer doesn't have slots."

I looked again at the wedding couple snow dome. I thought about Buddy's two dead wives, and wondered if the third was spending Christmas with her Circus Circus boyfriend, or if she'd moved on again. I wondered what my wife, and my kids, were doing for Christmas, and what my ex-wife was doing for Christmas. I thought about a Christmas long ago, when my kids still believed in Santa Claus.

"Shake one up. It's fun to shake them up."

I shook up the Statue of Liberty. It *was* fun.

"You know how they say each snow flake is different, that no two snowflakes are exactly the same. I'm talking about real snowflakes here," Buddy said.

"I've heard it."

"I wonder if these bone flakes work the same way," Buddy said. "I wonder if each tiny flake of bone is special in its own way."

I thought of all our failures, how each unique failure scraped just a little bone. I prayed I might learn something from these fresh, twirling flakes, before I was all out of bone.

"Buddy, what's going to happen to us?" I asked.

"More of the same, maybe," he reflected. "But maybe not."

Change, in our lives, had always instigated itself upon us, but surely there were ways to instigate ourselves upon change.

"Next time, you come to Detroit, Buddy."

"Yeah, that's probably a good idea."

"Promise me you'll come."

"Okay. Yes."

I thought I'd call my wife and kids when we got back to Buddy's apartment, before I went to bed and slept Christmas away. The tiny flakes of bone had settled to the bottom of each dome. Buddy picked them up, one by one, and shook: the snowstorm started all over again.

One Person's Garbage

I watched a 78 RCA Victrola go, a cedar hope chest, and then a pre-Xerox ditto machine. A chest of drawers. I stood, dressed in a smart calf-length skirt and sharp eggshell blouse, amid junky desks and stained mattresses and leather horse collars, like a sparkly backpacker in a shabby forest. The man held up a set of Santa and Mrs. Claus egg cups. That was the beginning.

From the back of the crowd I heard the man's microphoned voice rattling off strings of emphatic words that sounded like baseball cards in a bicycle tire's spokes—niceoldeggcups, stickersaysLefton, nocracksnochipsnodiscolouration. I pushed closer. About me, index cards shot up and fell. More baseball cards. More index cards. Auction card #107, without consulting me, went sky high.

The egg cups, relics even then, were exactly the kind I remember perched high in my best friend Mary Rose's basement. I wanted them. I didn't know why, but I wanted them. Real bad.

"Sold!!!"

There was no premeditation. That first time, Mary Rose asked me over on Christmas morning, as a playmate will do, and I accepted, as a play-mate will do. I knew, of course, what kind of house it was—*everybody* knew. Come Christmas, gawkers from near and far formed a slow, patient line around the perimeter. The yards, porches, roofs, garage, all the windows—*everything* was covered. Garland, snowmen, angels, Santa Clauses in a hundred sizes and shapes, reindeer, stars, Nativity scenes, Grinches and fairies, Tiny Tim and Mr. Scrooge, candy canes, wreaths, blinking lights and big lights and small lights and period lights, mistletoe. Red, yellow, green, blue, white, pink, aqua, lavender, beige, purple, gold, silver.

Sally and Martin—my mom and dad—deplored The Christmas House. In our community, and those nearby, the pilgrimage to The Christmas House ranked along with *It's a Wonderful Life* and Midnight Mass as can't-miss annual traditions. But Sally and Martin chose non-par-ticipation as their form of criticism, and partly through their efforts to ignore the hoopla they never connected Mary Rose to The Christmas House. I did not offer clarification. It was understood in our family that Christmas was a Christian holiday and, what's more, a bastion of the ugly commercialization of our society. We knew Christ as a fictional character, or at best a dubiously represented historical character, and we knew the idea of Christ had contributed to centuries of bloodshed, and we knew Christians tended toward the hypocritical.

So my duplicity began.

Opening the basement door was like entering a fantasy. Wreaths and lights and candles flashed. Elves hammered away at little workbenches—tap, tap tap, tap, tap tap. Santa bent at the waist to fill his bag. Reindeer hooves pawed an imaginary sky, and Rudolph's bright red nose lit the imaginary way. They even had this life-sized Mrs. Claus that squeaked "Cookies, Santa?"

A bushy Douglas fir anchored the basement's farthest corner. Prickly green needles drizzled on a pure white sheet spread over a plush blue carpet, and that cozy smell infected everything. A million wrapped packages bulged from under and around the tree's base, so many gifts you needed a sickle and hiking boots just to turn on the angel. The whole house was crazy that way—even the toilet paper holder was shaped like a wise man bearing a gift.

That first Christmas, and every Mary Rose Christmas thereafter, a single, glistening, bow-tied "Charity" present waited under the Culligans' Christmas tree. "Charity," Mrs. Culligan said, "this is your very own present. You leave it at our house and don't say a word, but it's yours."

It was our dirty secret.

The auctioneer held up a Happy Holidays Barbie. "Nice old doll," he said. "Who wants to give me ten? Ten dollars?" I pictured the doll in a glass display case, backlit to highlight her silver and green dress and accentuate the holly berry details. I mentally combined Happy Holidays Barbie with Christmas Morning Barbie and Holiday Hostess Barbie into a lovely little collection. I thought ahead, to how I would eventually get all the Barbie accessories: snow hats, sleighs, scarves, and…I had to have this doll.

The Collectibles Store Lady opened the bidding, and the Doll Lady upped it, and then back. The Daycare Teacher got into the fray. "Ten dollar bill, ten dollar bill, now eleven, now eleven, who'll give me twelve, twelve in the back, who'll go thirteen?"

I worked as a change management consultant. By the nature of my business, I associated only with wounded companies—those experiencing growing pains, or that had fallen behind the technological curve, or whose top-down managerial style no longer got results. I specialized in "mutual gains" bargaining between Union and Management. There were good days and bad days, but the atmosphere wore me down, and it had gotten to where the term "Win-Win" came off my tongue like so much insincere flattery.

Here, though…I wanted a Happy Holidays Barbie; these people

wanted to get rid of their Happy Holidays Barbie. This was a true win-win situation: one person's garbage was another person's treasure.

The Collectibles Store Lady dropped out—it was no good to her if she couldn't flip it for a profit—and then the Daycare Teacher fell away. I let it get to going twice before I raised my number. The surprised Doll Lady hesitated. She'd not anticipated a sniper, and her indecision, I could see, would keep her from going further. Then I spotted the pain-in-the-ass Jolly guy. He was an older but not old man, with a long, salt and pepper beard. Tiny spectacles. Rosy cheeks, like he'd had a few nips.

Doll Lady shook her head, "No." Jolly raised his index card. I raised mine. He raised his. These auctions were bloody, multi-front battles: just when you'd beaten back The Daycare Lady, a separate skirmish broke out with Jolly. Going once. Going twice. He laughed from the belly, which made me so angry. Jolly—he bid up auctions for sport. The auctioneer stood behind the podium and his assistant roamed the floor. The assistant crept closer; he stared right at me and flapped his fingers. Adrenalin, or maybe it was greed, took over. This thing I never before imagined I wanted, much less needed, pierced the core of my desires, until all my happiness seemed to depend on it. I blinked. The auctioneer said, "Did she do it?" I raised my index card. "She did it." Attention shifted to Jolly. Below the beard, it was all faded flannel and washed-out denim. He was ornamented in paint speckles, mud stains, probably hog shit. He bowed toward me: I had Happy Holidays Barbie.

Sally and Martin said just because they were Atheists didn't make us Atheists. They systematically exposed us to the spectrum of World religions. Buddhism. Islam. Unitarianism. Judaism. Christianity in its various strains. They even taught us about the Hare Krishnas. Ostensibly, we could, at a certain age, choose our own path, though there was little doubt we would do what they did, which was believe in nothing. You just don't see any 10-year-old kids choosing Catholicism over cartoons, or sacrificing Little League to hand out pamphlets at the airport, or willingly submitting to Hebrew lessons.

We lived in a small, somewhat rural community. It was an enclave for aging hippies like Sally and Martin, and our friends were mostly other aging hippies, who would come to the house with progeny named Joy, Hope, Sunny, or the occasional Destiny. We grew organic vegetables, made our own clothes, and used bikes as our main source of transportation. We were recycling when other people were still tossing garbage out their car windows.

We even did home schooling. Sally and Martin invented lesson plans based loosely on their radical vision of a free society. We exposed injustices ranging from Mistreatment of The American Indian, to Disastrous Environmental Policy Making, to Reaganomics: Fuck Us!

Our home life played against a backdrop of burning wood, bright wildflowers, glorious sunrises and breathtaking sunsets. We ate garden fresh vegetarian meals, often with friends and neighbors who habitually dropped by, in a house we never locked. We listened to NPR, discussed the news, and shared thoughts about literature, music and film. For all these simple pleasures I'm grateful.

But when it came to stuff, Mary Rose had it all.

I had very few friends, partly because I was shy but mostly because I had no classmates. I got lucky with Mary Rose; she and I had met at a swim class in town, and she'd adopted me. I held Mary Rose's real identity as a closely guarded secret. We would meet in town, or on the woodland path, at the pool, and sneak back to her place. I never invited her home. In debriefings to my parents, I'd edit out Mary Rose's name and most definitely her house. Mrs. Culligan was in on it: she'd drop me off down the road so that I could pretend to have walked home from somewhere else.

Judged by today's standards, it seems impossible that such significant portions of a young child's day—I was nine years old when I met Mary Rose—could go unscrutinized. But from early on, I was mostly self-sufficient. I walked or biked most places; I did chores or school work or played while Sally and Martin were away on important liberal matters; I went wherever I wanted, within reason, so long as I minded my curfews. Close to anything I wanted to do, such as a concert or trip to the library or the swim class, fell under the large umbrella of "home schooling." So while it was true that a simple, cursory background check would have squashed my merry Christmases, it was also true that such a thing simply didn't happen. And it was relatively easy to escape Christmas mornings, because in our house the day, unlike, say, Earth Day, didn't even register a spike.

At the Culligans', we never talked about religion in any way; I don't think God was really invited. Mrs. Culligan, who was a lumpy, cheerful, simple, right-out-of-the-catalogue mom, put me to work stringing popcorn. Mr. Culligan, a bearded engineer, had me test Christmas lights for the bad bulb. In my collage of memories, I'm opening a Holly Hobbit doll (*Cookies, Santa?*), and I'm opening Ants in Your Pants (*tap, tap tap, tap, tap tap*), and I'm opening the Charlie's Angels board game (*Cookies, Santa? Cookies, Santa?*). Mary Rose and I are hugging. We're awash in red, green and silver aluminum foil wrap. I'm high on sugar cookies. There's a log burning on the fire and *The Twelve Days of Christmas* playing on the hi-fi.

There's another part to my memories: the sadness at leaving my present behind, the conspiratorial tones on the way back to my house, and the incredible guilt. Mrs. Culligan would say, "Let's practice our story once." You have to understand. Sally and Martin believed what they preached, and they preached, from my infancy, an absolute contempt for material possessions. They hated the marketing, they hated the packaging, they hated the stores. They wanted me to find entertainment in my imagination, and through human interaction—not through *things*.

I always left the Culligans feeling: no more. Despite the pleasure, despite how much I wanted that day, despite the way my heart raced: no more.

The auctioneer worked his way down a series of long folding tables. He held up a turquoise pendant and said, "Start us off at ten, do we have ten?" He raised an indescribable mangle of rusted metal and declared, "Nice old you betcha. Give us three." Anything with even slight value got auctioned off separately, then the scattered junk went in blocks—choice of any item between two sticks, then everything left over. Sometimes they'd auction off a box filled with falling-apart spice tins, dog-eared paperback novels, old keys that went to who knows what doors, canning jars with no lids, drink cozies, and maybe a few dinged coasters.

I bid on a Punch and Judy Christmas tree ornament and a 1973 Holly Hobby Christmas commemorative plate, but really I lay in wait for the Charlie Brown Christmas figurines I'd sniffed out during the pre-auction viewing period. The night wore on. I preferred it when my most-sought-after items went late in the auction; by then a lot of people had blown their budget. The auctioneer held up the figurines and I made the rookie mistake of pouncing on the first bid, thus declaring my eagerness.

Jolly, who I hadn't noticed until then, planted himself opposite me across the folding tables. His merry face twinkled up the bid. I raised my index card, he raised his bearded smile. My head nodded, his face lit up. We went back and forth, like two foot soldiers stabbing at each other. Other bidders dropped out quickly.

The same people came week after week. The 78 LPs Woman had an old phonograph at home that spun 78 revolutions per minute, and she danced with her husband to Doris Day, Frank Sinatra and Dinah Shore. This Depression Glassware Guy could talk your ear off about a Dance of the Mermaids frosted red tumbler. You had to stand clear of The Camera Guy's elbows when a vintage Polaroid or an old Brownie box got held up. Others dealt in antiques or nostalgia, maybe had their own shop.

I didn't start out having a thing, but when bidding started on a Steinbach chimney sweep nutcracker, or a Swarovski crystal tree topper, or lighted reindeer yard art, my number shot up so fast I almost tore a rotator cuff.

Jolly tipped his John Deere hat, grinned, plucked his suspenders, lifted his beard, until the Charlie Brown figurines reached a ludicrous price. He stood perfectly still, and yet his animated, rosy face so sparkled he appeared to be in constant motion. What was Jolly's thing? He might have been a shop owner or a grandfather, or he might have done it just to taunt me. He looked like a farmer.

I wanted those figurines. I *really* wanted them. But—goddamn that Jolly!—I had to let him have this one.

I don't know how many years my secret Christmases at the Culligans' went on. It seemed like years and years. But maybe it was only four, perhaps five. Each one got increasingly elaborate. I remember dressing as The Silver Angel to hand out freshly baked cookies to The Christmas House pilgrims. I remember choir-like renditions of *Silent Night, Deck the Halls*, and *Here Comes Santa Claus*. I remember a candlelight vigil.

Mary Rose collected playmates. After a while, Ingrid Lundgren and Denise Talley and Kathy Olsen and Barbie McIntosh and Suzie Evensong were there. It got to be like a Christmas cult. After a while, I had my own shelf on which all the presents I'd gotten over the years accumulated. But ownership was a small part of it. I worked up a voracious appetite—not so much for the presents themselves but for the unwrapping of the presents.

I suppose, too, I knew I would get caught. At home, I began to feel the weight of my hypocrisy as I continued, without complaint, to take enthusiastic part in storytelling, singing, piano and guitar recitals, communal meals, bonfires, games of charades, long strolls and canoe trips, vegetable and fruit picking. It still gave me great satisfaction to impress my parents with cultural, historical and geopolitical knowledge. I wondered if I could stand the razor sharp edge of Sally and Martin's disappointment. I wondered if all their love was contingent on my ability to behave as they believed I should behave. My anxiety didn't manifest itself in quite so articulate terms, but more in a vision of their darkened, furled faces staring down at the top of my bandana-wrapped head.

Bigger was always better, and the year I'm thinking of a huge square box with my name on it sat under the tree. Mary Rose had many, many presents but none as big as mine. I retained, over those years, special status vis-à-vis the newer playmates—it was understood I was the best friend.

We drank hot chocolate. The moment approached. "Okay," Mrs. Culligan said. "Let's open."

It was a moment of almost pure insanity. The den, minus my present, turned white. A buzzing in my ears drowned out all sound. I massacred the bow, pulverized the Scotch tape, annihilated the aluminum wrap. I was a starving kid at a banquet; a virgin at an orgy.

There it was: an Easy-Bake Oven. My own Easy-Bake Oven!!! In the next moment the heat of desire turned into the heat of shame. I sat there in a sea of discarded wrap, surrounded by all these delightful presents and the smell of Christmas. I felt giddy and weak at the same time.

I told myself I would never do this again; but I *would* do it again, in the same exact way, with the same exact results, over and over. Until somebody stopped me.

A sense of urgency prevailed on that last auction night before the house shut down for the holidays. It was December, another dazzlingly bright day in a dazzlingly big place. The way it looked inside this warehouse, it might have been a carnival. There were stands set up to sell beverages, and corn dogs, and pork chops, and baked goods. After this, we would be into the wrapping and mailing stage, or, worse, the getting-something-*anything*-at-the-mall stage.

The tabletop was filled with goodies and the auction house with eager buyers. The 1928 Canada Dry Christmas advertisement I didn't think I'd get—the Advertising Freak would stop at nothing—but I had my heart set on the Department 56 snow babies and Mazda Bell lamps. Dick Tracy figural lights would have been nice, too. I'd take the Noel unicorn figurine at the right price.

In addition to being the only female consultant I was also basically the only single consultant, if you didn't count one retirement-aged widower. We worked like mad and I worked more than anybody else because otherwise they would blame it on inferior stamina, bachelorettehood, or—though they would never say it—cramps. My office was having another crisis—"the demands are going to be ridiculous, but if any team can meet this deadline it's this team"—which meant virtually no holiday.

I traveled a lot but was always in Houston on weekends, when the auctions were held. At first, I'd considered these weekend excursions a release, but soon they seemed more like binges, and then an addiction. Early in the week, I thumbed through collectible books I'd acquired. As the week progressed, I fantasized about all the things that might soon be my own. Friday nights, I could hardly sleep.

The egg cups and Happy Holidays Barbie and everything else went in The Closet. It was a walk-in hallway closet that I'd at first used as winter clothes storage. I stuffed one then another purchase into The Closet, gradually moved out all the winter clothes in order to dedicate it to my auction acquisitions. I kept cramming stuff in there and periodically taking it out to look at, like a photo album.

Jolly wandered into the barn. He wore rubber calf-high boots and walked with his feet at right angles to his body. His long salt-and-pepper beard and chin lifted in a smile. I nodded. He refused to acknowledge our acrimonious rivalry. He stretched his hands across his gigantic belly and surveyed the bustle, as if surveying his own kingdom.

He approached me, which had never happened. "I don't believe we've met," he said, holding out his hand. "I'm Mr. Heitzhusen. Everybody calls me Mr. H."

I refused to take his hand. "Charity Starbird."

He bowed. "Glad to meet you."

"Do you have it in for me?" I asked. "Is that it?"

He looked down his spectacles at me. He twinkled. "What is the thing that your heart most desires today?" he asked.

"If I tell you, will you lay off the bidding?" I asked. I batted my eyelids. Maybe I could seduce him out of outbidding me.

He leaned closer. He whispered, "If you tell me, then I will bid higher." He belly laughed. I don't know if he did it deliberately or not but I do know it sounded like, "Ho, ho, ho."

The auctioneer held up the first item, and we were parted by the crush of bodies. Everybody tried to get an angle on the item, tried to get in position where they could monitor the rhythm of the bidding. Jolly actually outbid the Advertising Freak on Canada Dry Christmas. He outbid me on the Noel unicorns. An item went up, frenzied bidding ensued, another item went up, more frenzied bidding, and so forth.

When the doll went up for bid, I hadn't a notion to bid on it. "Nice old dolls," the auctioneer said. "Who'll give me five dollars?"

I fought through the crowd. You never want to impulse bid—the thing to do is thoroughly examine the item beforehand, mentally calculate its true value, then set an upper limit on the price you'll pay—but I'd apparently missed this during the viewing period. Now, frantically, I looked closer: yes, it was a *Mister Magoo's Christmas Carol* doll.

Mrs. Culligan would call a special session to watch the movie on local television; it was a musical adaptation of Dickens's *A Christmas Carol* and featured, I think for the first time, the bumbling, near-blind animated character voiced by Jim Backus. Mary Rose and I would bump around the basement, pretending to look for our lost glasses. Then we'd burst out laughing.

"A hundred dollars," I screamed. Confused and irritated heads turned toward me. The bidding had only reached twenty-five dollars, and I'd senselessly quadrupled the going price. Not even Jolly, who now looked more curiously at the doll, would stand in my way. It was clear to all I would match any price. The auctioneer looked around. "Going once…" I felt such a sense of elation, I can hardly describe. The wheezy, battered, pale doll was almost mine. "Going twice…." Like always, this thing seemed like the crowning jewel of all things, a prize to end all prizes. "Gone."

On the final, fatal Culligan Christmas, the celebration had reached a high-pitched fever. That year, they hired a Santa Claus to come to the house. He made this fabulous entrance on what I now know couldn't have been real reindeer but to this day don't know what else they might have been. Sally showed up in the middle of all this. I was sitting in a pile of discarded wrapping paper—pink and yellow checkered paper, silver diamond-covered paper, tan teddy bear paper, black and red striped paper—with my unopened present on my lap. She walked with purpose from one side of the room to the other. She stepped over bows (*Cookies, Santa?*) and gift tags (*tap, tap tap, tap, tap tap*) and mauled boxes (*Cookies, Santa? Cookies, Santa? Cookies, Santa?*).

"Come on, we're going," she said, and grabbed my hand. My present fell to the floor. Suzie and Karen dove at it, like soldiers going for the dead man's pack. Mrs. Culligan stuffed her hands down in her apron pockets. She started to wave, then dropped her hand. Mary Rose looked up. At the same moment, a mechanical monkey beat on its drum, and she turned away.

I woke before dawn and could not fall back asleep. I never remember a time when I believed in Santa Claus. Maybe nobody does. It's impossible, I suppose, to reconstruct naiveté. Sally and Martin believed that honesty equaled respect, and so early on they explained the myth of Santa Claus, or St. Nicholas, and even provided cultural and religious context for the stories. There must have been some moment in my infancy, though, when I did believe—when I thought as my friends thought.

I lay there. I shut my eyes, I opened my eyes, shut them again. I craved the jubilation I'd gotten in my toes, the dreams, the piercing sensation that the day was special. I pulled down the blanket, lifted my aging body from bed, put on my housecoat, and pulled back the curtain to watch the sun rearing its fiery head. I felt a little lost, or incomplete.

I curled up in my armchair with time sheets and expense reports in one hand and a mug of hot chocolate in the other. I dozed a little. A solitary Christmas morning. Outside, the sun heated a mild Texas day. I longed just then for human voices—maybe even my own. I thought about calling Sally and Martin—not about Christmas, but just to call. I never complained about my lost Mary Rose Christmases. In fact, I agreed almost wholeheartedly with Martin and Sally's assessment of the situation. I wanted, naturally, to please them. But I believe, all these years later, that my acquiescence, my inability to articulate a contrary belief system, was what caused me to drift, emotionally and physically, from my family, and that we're all worse off for it.

I refilled my hot cocoa and fumbled through paperwork, The Closet filled with Christmas cheer but the house cranky except for a brilliantly decorated tree that housed no presents.

The bell rang. I welcomed the intrusion, any intrusion, though I couldn't imagine what it might be.

Jolly stood on my Welcome mat, carrying shopping bags in both hands. He looked happy and confident. "Merry Christmas, Charity," he said.

"Um, hello…Mr. H," I said. I cracked open the screen door and shook his hand. I'd hated him—not actively, but still—until that very moment. You couldn't call somebody Mr. H and hate him at the same time, especially not on Christmas.

The sun—even the sun seemed bigger in Texas—fell quickly in the swirling distant sky. My body blocked the entrance. I opened my hip and shoulder slightly—I was thinking about letting him in. What was preventing me? Here was an older man, who looked a lot like a farmer and a little like Santa Claus, arriving unannounced at my doorstep on Christmas Day. What could he possibly be doing at my doorstep?

I still had the mug of hot cocoa in my hand. "Would you like some hot chocolate, or something? Come in."

He removed his rubber boots and left them outside on the Welcome mat. He wore wooly gray socks. He seemed to accept the quiet as a matter of course. Jolly appeared somehow to have access to my loneliness, to a despair and emptiness I hadn't admitted even to myself. How did he know? I wondered what telltale signs I displayed, the difference between what I'd projected and what others had perceived.

Mr. H lugged his shopping bags over to the tree. He dropped to his beaten, washed-out, denim-clad knees. He pulled out a wrapped rectangular box. He peered over his spectacles. He placed the present on top of the dried needles that had settled on top of my own white sheet. He pulled more and more presents from the bags, until an arc formed around the base of the tree.

He rose. He settled into an old rocking chair that nobody ever sat on. His face twinkled, as if he were totally amused with himself. "Open," he said.

I pulled my housecoat tighter. I smiled. "For me?" I asked.

"Merry Christmas," he said. He sat, comfortable as could be, in that rocking chair. I tentatively stepped over to the tree. I dropped to my bare knees. I looked at him. "I…well, I didn't get you anything," I said. He laughed. I laughed. He laughed back.

I tore at the paper. The Charlie Brown figurines. It was one of the many, many items Mr. H had outbid me on over the course of the past year. I looked up at him. "Thanks," I said. I had so many questions, I didn't know where to begin. He sipped his hot cocoa. He asked, "Got anything I might put in this cup, to give it a little more holiday spirit?"

"There's Schnapps in the kitchen cabinet," I said. He bowed. He helped himself while I tore open more boxes. Star Wars Christmas collectibles—Yoda and Vader as Santa. Avon holiday plates. A bunch of vintage Christmas LPs. All were items he'd outbid me on, and which, at the time, had infuriated me.

Mr. H polished off a half-pint of Schnapps with his hot cocoa, and I joined him. I found myself surprisingly touched, almost weepy. That was what I'd wanted and never gotten from my parents: a present I wanted, just because I wanted it.

"Are there other auction goers on your shopping list?" I asked.

"Some from the auction. Some from the market where I shop. Some from the orphanage and the old people's home. Some from the Little League team I sponsor."

Suddenly, Mr. H struck me as a fascinating, almost mystical character.

"Are you married?" I asked.

"Not really," he said.

"Do you believe in God?" I asked.

"I do, in my own way, which I suppose is how all believers believe," he said.

I noticed Jolly scrutinizing the decor. His face grew cherry red as he methodically worked his way through the Schnapps. "Where is everything?" he asked, genuinely puzzled, genuinely interested. I felt I should be sitting on his lap.

I wrung my hands. I'd been aware for some time that I had this Christmas collection, and it bothered me that there was no end game, that in obsessing over a theme without any expression of the theme that my interest amounted to nothing more than a fetish. It embarrassed me some.

I tilted my head toward The Closet. Jolly lifted a brow, as if to say,

"There?" I nodded. He stood, unsteadily. He opened the door. "My! My, my, my!!!" he exclaimed.

He rolled up his sleeves and began pulling things out, one at a time. He paused to admire each item. "She's a beauty," he said. Or, "Lovely, just lovely!"

"We need thumb tacks, tape, a hammer and some nails," he said. "We need a foot ladder." I scurried about, gathering the materials.

Jolly worked like a plowman at harvest time. He banged and straightened and we hung and arranged, all the while chattering happily. Jolly gave me various installation tips, recommended materials, offered design and cleaning advice, in general tutored me on the ways and means to own and operate the area's newest Christmas House.

"Twist the garland, like so," Jolly coached, "and it will stay better."

"Do you think I should keep all the Disney figures together or mix and match with some of the others?" I asked.

"You try out one, then the other," Jolly said. "This is a work in progress."

The metamorphosis involved not just the house. The infusion of light, color and good cheer reached deep down in parts of me that had lain dormant, ignored or just underused. The house, and me with it, seemed, suddenly, to vibrate. It was like a dusty old piano springing to life beneath the nimble fingers of a skilled jazz pianist.

Darkness descended rapidly, as it did that time of year. I stood with Jolly at the front window. The front yard disappeared under a cloak of deep dark blue as an underworld of owls and bats and mice rustled about. Jolly said, "Okay, throw her!" I flipped a switch and everything suddenly came alive with color and motion.

I silently took it all in, shoulder to shoulder with this man I'd hardly known four hours ago. A red and green smudge reflected off the window onto my housecoat, and a twirling star hit my face.

Whatever's Left of Normal

I sat with my back against a Humvee's tire, smoking a Kool cigarette I'd learned to love here. A notebook and pen lay on my lap. Most of the men emailed home, but I found romance in such Hollywood war images as the hand-written letter. My body was on Kosovo time, my mind on New England time. I thought about what Mom was doing now, and P.J., and Angelina, and my little niece and nephew. Christmas evening here, Christmas morning there. Who got what? Would Kelsey's face squinch with delight when she opened the doll I'd bought her in Frankfurt? Would little P.J. Junior whoop when he got the electric loco, class E44, from Fleischmann's original HO range? Me: Uncle Luke. I thought about how it was time to get started on my own family.

The mountain range on the horizon, dabbed with snow, seemed strangely blue this evening. The misty air stung my cheeks and hands, and I followed the sweep of wind across stubborn wildflowers to my tent's flapping doorway. The diesel generators made an infernal racket I hardly noticed anymore. Small arms and artillery fire popped in the distance.

I worked five a.m. to five p.m., seven days a week. It felt especially good, Christmas day, to be done. The mood was light, if not festive, and I could hear the ping-pong ball going back and forth inside the makeshift rec center. Clack-Clack, clack-clack; clack-clack, clack-clack; WHAP; clickety-clickety-clickety-clickety. We were waiting on the big turkey dinner. I thought about life beyond the Constantine wires that defined our camp. I still thought of it as Yugoslavia, and visualized the map the way it was before borders and identities changed and changed and changed again. I knew so little about the people. Were they Christians? Muslims? Jews?

Was there a Kosovo Christmas happening somewhere just beyond my grasp?

Jones bummed a menthol cigarette. A football skipped past. Pritchard approached. "I got a three-hour to Camp Bon-Steel. Who wants what?" Men scurried about for money stashes and called out beef jerky, soda pop, pizza, tacos, cigarettes, even shaving cream. Then Roberts came over to give me shit.

"What are you doing?" he asked. "Designing the division Christmas cards?"

I'd reenlisted at age 31 on the urging of an aggressive, persuasive recruiter, who I never saw again after I'd signed the forms. He'd promised me an e-4 pay rate, choice of duty stations, and, most importantly, graphic design experience. Graphic design was my MOS—military occupation specialty. As a reserve, I had input data, fetched coffee, done vehicle maintenance; anything but graphic design work. I thought for sure—and my recruiter *promised*—active duty would be different.

That first day—this was in Darmstock, Germany—Platoon Sgt. Ramsey gave me my first assignment: kill the rats in an old Nazi storeroom. I thought there was a mistake. Once Sgt. Ramsey realized I was The Graphic Designer he would assign me a more suitable job, like laying out the *Stars & Stripes*. "Sergeant," I said, "I'm reporting for graphic design duty."

He looked me over. He got right up in my face. He said, "Specialist Fiori, you want to design something? Design a way to kill those rats, and do it NOW, Fiori, do it NOW."

"I'm designing a way to make you shut the fuck up," I told Roberts. It was all good-natured. Me and Roberts had become best friends, partly because we were about the same age, which was quite a bit older than your average enlisted man, and partly because he was also a graphic designer killing rats with a gas can and pitch fork. We'd shipped out together— from Darmstock we'd ridden the train in full battle gear to Italy, then bused through Bosnia all the way here, to the old Macedonia border. You never forget the men you were with when the orders came.

Men were laughing. The ping-pong ball was clack-clacking. The generator whirred and wind wisped. Guns pop popped.

That was when the mine exploded.

Mines littered that country like stones—along footpaths, under bridges, in meadows. From time to time, we heard an explosion. This one was close, and so had a startling, almost awe-inspiring effect. Then came the whimper. It was carried along on the wake of the explosion, and we all heard it at the same time. It sounded like a wounded animal—a bird, maybe, or a baby moose. It was a cry for help that seemed resigned not to be helped.

"Ummmm, Mah. Ummmm, Mah Mah."

They were actually words in a crazy Slavic language, but to our American ears they came across as a long, agonizing wail. I stood, still holding my Kool. Jones and Roberts took a few careful steps toward the wailing. The tents that served as our barracks emptied, at first just a few soldiers, then a few more, and then the deuce-and-a-halves we'd converted to offices emptied, a few on-duty specialists, then a few more, until, finally, we all stood there, frozen. MUUUHHHHHHH, MUUUUUHHHHHHHHHH. A-OOOOGLLAAA."

John Adamski, affectionately known as Ski, said what we all were thinking. "That's a little girl out there," Ski said. "She's out there."

None of us wanted to die. Or, I should say, I didn't want to die; I didn't know for certain about anybody else. I'd always considered myself courageous, but what did I know of courage? What did any of us know about courage? I was in the army to pad my resume, maybe visit Paris or Prague or Munich. Had I any notion I'd be shipped off to war, or *peace-keeping*, as they were calling it…no. No, sir.

In those very first moments after the wailing started, a clatter of action plans were formed. The loudest men, notably Jenkins, insisted we save the little girl. In the army, leadership worked a little like this—the loudest, brashest men pulled the quieter, indecisive men with them. Who, anyway, wanted to be known as a guy on the side of leaving the little girl out there? The cries continued. The men wanted to do something. I wanted to do something. I found myself face-to-face with Roberts, and I whispered, "What do you think?"

Here the risk and the reward were clearly outlined: our lives to save the life of a young girl entirely unknown to us except by her cries. There was the chance, too, we'd all get blown up, and then it would be another in a long line of futile heroism.

Roberts shook his head, like "Tough call." Then he shook his head again. "What kind of men would we be?"

Six of us, with Jenkins leading the way, made for the wails. We started at a trot, slowed to a fast walk as we approached the Constantine wires. We ran straight into the gun barrel of this MP, I think his name was Phillips, a 19-year-old kid, which all the MPs were, more or less. "Get back," he said, then cocked his rifle. "Do NOT cross the wire."

His nose twitched, and he blinked. He kept the barrel trained on Jenkins. A barely comprehensible fracas ensued—several men loudly arguing their point; several other men trying to hold back the most aggressive men; me and Roberts finally running off to get the Lt. Colonel.

We found Lt. Colonel McNamara, the highest-ranking officer at our Node Center, halfway between his office and the MP station. We ran alongside him, spouting details. He stopped. "Specialist Fiori, Specialist Roberts, *I* am now in control of the situation. Go eat your turkey dinners; I *will* handle the situation."

One opinion mattered in that world, on that day, and that was Lt. Colonel McNamara's. Technically, in an emergency situation, the green, pimply-faced MPs, who took their orders from the top, outranked the highest-ranked officer. In reality, the MPs would go along with whatever Lt. Colonel McNamara decided.

We gathered. Lt. Colonel McNamara listened briefly to our pleas, but the wails were the only hard facts we had. He could hear them as clearly as we could. "Nobody, I repeat NOBODY, is to lift a finger until I get an engineer here to clear a path," he said. Ours was a military intelligence brigade attached to a signal battalion. Our purpose, primarily, was to erect and maintain a cell tower to facilitate communication throughout the mountainside with all the other cell towers, from the front lines down. There was no engineer on site, maybe not one for many, many miles. "Everybody that is on duty, go do your jobs. Everybody else, go eat your Christmas dinners."

She must have been injured, and my hope was she couldn't move. Because if she could, another mine would surely get her. Then again, she was in pain, probably bleeding, and that might be a worse way to die still.

We returned to the spot just outside the makeshift rec center. The ping-pong balls, not to mention the laughter, had gone silent. I looked down at my Kool. I stared at the Humvee. Nothing seemed as it was just minutes ago. I couldn't stand. I couldn't sit. I stooped into a crouch, rocked back and forth on my heels, like a dog waiting for a command. Those wails now came in steady one and a half minute intervals, like the hiccups. In between wails there was nothing to do but anticipate the next wail, and pray for the wails to go away.

Nobody went to dinner. That was our homage to that little suffering girl: we ignored the turkey and the cranberry sauce and all the other special food we never got in that place. I picked up my notepad, my pen. My mind went to my own childhood, and more so than ever I wished to dear God I could just get home.

We grew up, me and my little brother, in a single parent home in which Santa Claus ostensibly made all the big decisions. Mom played Good Santa to the fictional Santa's Bad Santa. We really truly believed this for more years than I care to admit.

"That's not going to play well to Santa," Mom would say when I'd broken a neighbor's window or P.J. had sassed back.

"Will he take away TV privileges?" I'd ask.

"He might just do that. He might do worse."

We'd cower at the very thought of Santa Claus, who, true to his legendary persona, knew every little thing we did, as we did it. I can't remember exactly what I pictured, but it included Mom in her work skirt in private conference with the red-suited, bearded man others knew as jolly but whom I knew as a strict disciplinarian.

"I'll see what I can do," Mom would say. "He might budge on this one, if you…can I tell him you'll pay for the window out of your allowance and make an apology to Mr. Rudy?"

"Tell him that," I'd say.

"I can only tell him what I know to be true," she'd say. "Is that your intention?"

"Yes, ma'am, it is, you can tell Santa Claus that, truthfully."

It was always presented this way: Mom as an intermediary between us and Santa. Mom won concessions, or else passed down the harsher sentences. "I'm afraid Santa insists you give up after-school playtime for the next two weeks," she'd say.

"Is it the grades issue?" I'd ask.

"That's it, exactly. I was in there swinging for you, I told him you were going to try harder and not let your attention wander during math lessons anymore. He said the proof is in the pudding."

"Santa said the proof was in the pudding?"

"What he meant was, he'd believe it when he saw improved marks on your next report card."

Christmas in that tiny, over-mortgaged house absolutely vibrated with the roar of our model train set. Each year, our model train village and model train tracks, all the little plastic boulders and trees and logging supplies, all the scale bridges and depots, grew and grew and grew, until it seemed to take over the house. Our father, who died in our infancy of lung cancer, was a railroad man. Christmas mornings, gathered around the old and new train parts, the whistles and choo choos screaming, Mom would tell us about our dead dad. He was a hero to us.

God, Mom was beautiful. And still young. She worked in a department store full-time and also took on laundering work at home on the weekends. I suppose she had no time to find a new husband, or else didn't believe in second chances that way. We were happy; that was the way I remembered it.

"Mark my words," Roberts said. He startled me. I'd been anticipating that next wail. There it came: AAAACCCCH OOOOO MAAAAH. We both stopped to let it pass, like the roar of one of those tiny trains. "That girl's going to be long dead before the engineer gets here."

Jenkins, who was still in a lather, stomped toward us. "I ain't letting this happen, I don't give a good goddamn what the fuck Fuck Face MP says."

"Orders," Jones corrected.

"Order's an order only if men obey it," Jenkins said. "And if Fuck Face tells me to stay, I sure as fuck am going to go anyway."

The tenor in his voice clearly invited the rest of us to revolt. The insinuation was, right was right, wrong was wrong, and we were morally obligated to save the girl. I wasn't as sure. There might be other mines. It might be a trap. Specialist Schramm, this pint-sized sexy intelligence woman, said, "I'm in, if y'all are in."

Was it so clear? I know it was chauvinist of me, but I thought of Schramm's lovely, hard, feminine body blown to pieces. I know it was selfish of me, but I pictured my own body similarly scattered. Either way, it was as much about us as the girl: what might happen to us if we attempted a rescue, how might we feel about ourselves if we didn't.

Sometimes doing nothing is doing something. And that was what we did, all of us, including Jenkins: nothing. I lit a Kool off the nub of another Kool.

My great grandfather, also a railroad man, had started the model train collection. One of my few clear Dad memories was of a Christmas when I was only a couple of years old and P.J. must have been a baby. He said with pride, "This is fourth generation now, and when you hand it off to your first son, it'll be fifth generation." Pride filled the room.

Once P.J. got mad and threw an antique boxcar to the floor. Mom quietly picked up the pieces. P.J. and I were too immature to be explicitly aware of the trains as a sentimental and metaphorical link to our past. Trains were fun. They were silver and sometimes green and gold, and they could go pretty fast around bends if you set the track up just right. At the same time, we knew intuitively that those trains were extremely important. If Mom meant to cry, she didn't show it. She said, "I'm going to have to tell Santa about this." P.J. pleaded for her not to, that he was sorry as soon as he'd done it. She just shook her head solemnly. "He's gonna ask."

When Mom went away, ostensibly to meet Santa Claus, P.J. and I sat around the house, alone. We debated what would happen.

"Santa Claus might personally come over here and spank your bottom," I guessed.

"That might be alright," P.J. mused.

My own anxiety, I remember it clearly all these years later, was as pronounced as P.J.'s, for I knew, subconsciously, we were in it together, and a ruined Christmas was a ruined Christmas for everybody.

The door opened and closed and we waited, our tiny faces twisted in nerves. It wasn't until many years later I'd learn that Mom would walk down to the park, smoke a cigarette, and collect her wits, before turning around and coming back home.

"I'm not sure how that went," Mom said.

The wail sounded again. ACCCCHOOOO MAAAH HAAA MAAA. It seemed to have lost its intensity, or else I'd gotten used to it. I had a clear picture of the girl in my head—local children sometimes came to the edge of the wire, from nearby villages or farms or wherever. They'd gawk at us American soldiers like we were right out of an action comic book. In my head was a girl I'd seen on two different occasions. She had a sweet cherry face that I imagined drenched in tears and dirt and blood, and I imagined her dark hair with stringy bangs, a checkered skirt all muddied and tiny fingers curled into a fierce ball.

The locals, it occurred to me, had made it safely here; we would probably make it safely there. *Probably.*

"Bouncing Betty," Roberts guessed.

A Bouncing Betty was a mine designed to explode at exactly crotch height to the average American soldier. It castrated rather than killed. In one theory of war, it was better to inflict agonizing wounds than to kill. This way, you'd still knock out the first soldier, plus it would require two more soldiers to remove the first soldier, plus the human and financial cost of medical attention. And, of course, the damage to morale.

"You heard the explosion," Ski said. "Anti-tank, no doubt."

"AAAAH CHOOO MAAAHHH OOOH."

Now it *was* wailing, not speaking. Wailing, in Serbian, or whatever language it was, somehow resonated fuller, deeper, more profoundly than English. It seemed like a hard-won sadness. Jenkins paused to let the scream die. He tried to start again, but just shook his head.

I flopped down against the Humvee's tire. I lit another Kool.

One Christmas, I woke to a sound I was sure was a clumsy, or maybe tipsy, Santa Claus struggling down the chimney. I jumped down from my top bunk. I roused P.J. "P.J.," I whispered. "Santa Claus!!!" He rose. Within seconds, he'd confirmed my suspicions. "It's HIM," he said. I whispered, "Mom, Mom, Mom: Santa Claus!!!" while at the same time P.J. whispered, "Mom, MOM, SANTA CLAUS, MOM!!!" Our whispers turned louder, a little louder, until, as we simultaneously burst through Mom's bedroom door, we were shouting. MOM!!! SANTA CLAUS IS HERE!!! She was already awake. She was sitting straight up in bed, holding the phone in one hand and a broom in the other. We jumped into bed on either side of her. "Sssshhh," she said, holding a finger to her mouth. "It's early yet for Santa Claus; it's not like him to veer from his schedule."

After ruling out a number of possibilities that in retrospect were all ridiculous, we discovered the source of the banging. It was a bat. In the attic. P.J., the braver of us two, grabbed the broom and said, "I'll do it." But Mom said, "Put the broom away, son."

We could easily have killed that stupid, blind, scary rodent. Mom wouldn't have it. She said, "Santa wouldn't like hearing we killed one of God's creatures, on today of all days." We dodged that crazy bat for what seemed hours. It flew back and forth, back and forth, while we, after

careful strategy sessions in the stairwell below, executed a plan to open all the attic windows, which proved very difficult to accomplish in the ten or fifteen second intervals between crazy, squeaking flights. Then, with windows open at either terminal of the wacky, zigzagged flight pattern, the bat refused our invitation to freedom. It knocked against the wall above one window, turned around, knocked against the wall above the other window. Finally, we got an old sheet out of storage. The three of us, Mom on one side and me and my brother on the other, stretched it the length and height of the attic, so that the bat had nowhere to go but straight into the white linen. We folded the sheet into a temporary cage. With the black bat beating blindly against the white sheet, we ran—screaming, all of us, in horror of being bitten or even touched by this wild animal—to the open window and chucked out the bat, sheet and all.

The bat flew away as the sheet dropped to the ground. We all cheered and hugged. I remember looking out into our backyard at the white that was the prettiest white I knew. The New England landscape had always seemed to me crystal to every place else's glass.

A Kool cigarette burned slowly to its nub. I'd gone through a whole pack, though it seemed to me the first cigarette of the day. In that silence there, it seemed I could never again enjoy that burning taste of menthol in my throat, or anything else for that matter.

I looked at my hardly started letter to Mom. I'd been telling her about the usual things here, and asking about the usual things there. I hunched over my pad. I fell back to recording little details—weather, food, rumors about travel and promotion and leave. Every time I tried to take up the subject of the little girl dying, I just couldn't do it. For the first time I understood why you rarely heard veterans speak of their war experiences. The thing you most wanted was to leave that there, and go back to whatever was left of normal.

The wails tapered off, then stopped. I heard, for the first time in an hour, the wind and the artillery fire and the generator. We kept our eyes peeled on the road that would carry the engineer, ignoring what we all knew, and eventually a Humvee came speeding our way. We stood. The engineer cleared a path, and then Ski and Jenkins went out there with a stretcher. They came back with a limp, lifeless little body that looked peaceful all out of proportion to what we knew was her end.

That Christmas morning, the Christmas morning of the bat, we were particularly exhilarated. Not only had we defeated the enemy—that stupid, dangerous bat—but at the same time we'd saved the enemy. Later that morning—Mom had forced us back into bed—we ran downstairs to find the train set up and running all through the living room.

This Christmas morning, the Christmas morning of the little wailing girl, we were numb. We had not defeated nor saved the enemy, and suddenly it seemed obvious that you could rarely have it both ways. You either saved yourself, or you saved the enemy. Those caught in the crossfire, which was most everybody, were worse off still.

Christmas Releases

I logged on: the room was a total snorefest. It was only nine o'clock, meaning half the regulars were still asleep or else doing the whole Santa Claus thing. That was true, I knew, for Tigger22, who had a much younger sister.

Boys immediately tried getting in my box. "Are you wet, JAP?" "What are you wearing?" "I'm SO horny." Like I sat around all day in a puddle of my own juices, wearing six-inch stilettos, a red teddy and fishnet stockings. I shooed away several pervs, ignored the rest, and typed a message in the big room, "Hi ALL."

"Merry Christmas!!!" some asshole named HungBuck18 responded.

"Which part of Jewish don't you get?" I typed.

"Christmas is for everybody!!!" some other asshole, SoccerStud, joined in.

"It is NOT," I returned. "It's only for Christians."

"The SPIRIT of it is for everybody," a third asshole, HappyShorts85, interjected.

I typed, "JAP15 sticks a Menorah up HappyShorts's ass."

That drew a few LMAOs and LOLs. New guests logged in all the while: PocketRocket, EarlyMorningRiser, 10INCowboy, KittyLicker, BushWhacker. Boys felt this compulsion to advertise 1. their erections, 2. the size of their penises, 3. their keenness for sex, mistakenly thinking women, like themselves, merely required a warm, willing, anatomically impressive body. There were a lot of high schoolers, like me, but also a bunch of old married pervs and some old desperate sluts (also, usually, married) (also, usually, lesbians) and then a handful of little kids, some just ten or eleven years old.

Still no Tigger22. His real name was Paul something Italian, and we had plans to meet today—to fuck, I guess. At least, we'd been seriously cybering for, like, a year, and we'd told each other everything we wanted to do to and have done by each other, and he was sneaking out on Christmas dinner to do this.

HarryPotter22, Paris, Hottie and more regulars popped in. Random guests kept volleying private messages asking me for phone sex or to meet—I mean, they didn't even know what I looked like or how old I was, or anything, and I think if I said YES they'd actually grab some condoms, start the car, and drive like hell to get here. Why did everybody think being in a chat room was an invitation to be totally unedited, even though it was, in a way?

"Has anybody seen Tigger?" I wrote. Bunch of nopes. Tigger lived like three subdivisions over, and we were probably going to meet at the movie theatre, where I was going to go anyway on Christmas Day. After that…we weren't positive, but we had talked about a bunch of places we could go to be alone. Paul was a total Italian Catholic—my mom and dad would have instantly disowned me. But he was sweet and funny and kind of smart. He didn't like sports or reality TV. He hated Bush.

I was a virgin, but nobody believed that because I was, like, a super sexual person, I mean, amazingly sexual; it was only that I hadn't actually had sex yet, if that made sense. Most of my friends had—nearly all, in fact. Even the Future Librarians of America crowd. I was too picky, I think, or too Jewish, or not Jewish enough, I'm not sure, but I'd had plenty of chances and passed. I mean, it was nothing but chances. If you were even vaguely hot, which I was, just about any guy would fuck you, didn't matter if they were young or old, married or single, whatever, as long as they figured they wouldn't get caught by whoever wasn't supposed to find out. Knowing that made it a little harder, not that I was against fucking for fucking's sake, but, you know, I wondered sometimes if there was a point to it all. There didn't have to be, but if there was I wanted to know it going in, not later.

I emailed Tigger: "Where are you? I'm going to breakfast, BRB."

I went downstairs. My dad was eating bagels and lox and reading the *Wall Street Journal*. He was the most Jewish dad I knew.

"Good morning, sleepyhead," he crooned.

I kissed him on the cheek and made a beeline for the Apple Jacks. I joined Mom outside. She was reading a self-help book in the rock garden. We had the typical Arizona backyard: cactuses, bird feeders, a pool, rocks everywhere, a clay-colored wall blocking any view that was left after they built 46 Wal-Marts and a thousand identical houses. "Hey," I said, and plopped down on the wicker chair.

"We have reservations at Big Wa's for one-thirty," Mom said.

"Oh, fun," I said. I was so sick of our Chinese dinner tradition. "Can't we try anything new for once?"

"You like Big Wa's. Plus they have a special Christmas menu."

We had Jewish friends and non-Jewish friends—Dad called them Gentiles—and we always went to Big Wa's with some of our Jewish friends, either the Kaufmans or Goldblatts or both. Afterward the adults played cards and the kids went to a movie. I was sort of between childhood and adulthood, but if *50 First Dates* meant one thing and Pinochle another, then I was definitely still a kid.

"Oh, Dana," Mom sighed. Big Wa's was okay, but it was crazy with Jews on Christmas—it got loud and smoky.

When I got back upstairs, there was Tigger. "Good morning," he typed.

125

I LOVED Tigger. It was the little things, like not saying Merry Christmas to a Jew. Another thing: he punctuated. Almost everybody else was just so lazy; pretty much nobody bothered to spell right or capitalize or end sentences with a period. Tigger's neatness showed a conscientious side; it showed respect for his correspondent.

"Merry X-Mas," I typed. "Was Santa good to you?"

"I got like 100 pair of socks," he wrote. "We're going to my Uncle Frank's at two. He lives in Mesa. I'll say I'm sick. They won't be back until late tonight; you could maybe even come here."

Neither of us drove, which meant we were slaves to geography. But we were both close enough to the movie theatre to meet there. That was how we first started chatting: the freaky fact that we were both from Casa Grande. I mean, it wasn't a local chat room; there were people from Australia, England, Scotland, and all over the U.S.—Dallas, Detroit, Atlanta—just about anyplace but Casa Grande.

Tigger wrote, "Dana, are you sure about today?" Meanwhile, some lezzie was trying to get into my box—"Are you bi?"—so I put on the p.m. block.

"I'm in," I said. We decided to definitely meet at the movie theatre, just before four.

I got through an hour and a half at Big Wa's (a Gi-Normous table of hungry Jews), and managed to discourage Laurel Goldblatt and Rachel Kaufman from meeting me at the movies. I obsessively thought about Tigger—it was hard to believe we'd never met. I thought about him sometimes as I watched out the school bus window—where was he? what was he doing now?—and actually smiled when I remembered something funny or cute he'd said. We'd sent photos, talked on our mobiles, chatted and emailed. Had it really been a year? Had it really been *only* a year?

I trudged along the diagonal dirt path that cut across two idle construction zones. I crossed the mall parking lot (well, it wasn't a full-blown shopping mall, but a strip mall like everywhere along Florence Boulevard from the highway to downtown), to the front entrance of the worst movie theater ever. I LOVED old movies (not like *Fargo*, though I loved that, too, but old old movies, like *Psycho* and *Breakfast at Tiffany's*), and I LOVED old theatres, but we had neither here. No: we had the worst six-screen theatre EVER. An enormous Indian family (not enormous like fat, enormous like there were a lot of them) (not American Indian, but Indian Indian) ran the place. A girl my age with a baby took tickets (they were ripped-up pieces of printer paper); teenaged sisters and brothers ran concessions and cleaned up (barely); the mom and dad walked around basically scowling.

The lobby, if you could even call it that, reeked of curry. The concrete slabs they called floors were a total Goo Alert. All the signs, including the "marquee" signs over individual theatres, were handmade with pieces of cardboard and black Sharpies. I looked for Tigger; I wasn't positive I'd recognize him. It was a big Jew Fest, like you'd expect, but there were a few scattered non-Jews, plus a bunch of Indians that didn't look necessarily related to the Indian owners. No Tigger. It was odd that I still mostly thought of him as Tigger; I wondered if I'd start to think of him as Paul after we'd had sex.

I peeked in a few theatres. We had no plans to actually see a movie, but I had nothing better to do than look around. Speakers stood on cardboard boxes near the entrances. The reupholstered chairs bled stuffing. It was really hot and not dark enough. You could hear dialogue from the other five crap movies in whichever crap movie was left over.

I stepped back into the lobby. I tried to look like I was waiting for somebody, so that 1. The Indian family wouldn't think I was trying to sneak in and 2. Tigger would guess I was JAP15.

The four o'clock movie started. The lobby emptied. I bought a Gi-Normous box of popcorn and a drum of Coke, stepped out the back door. It was sort of an alley, or a parking lot, or a construction zone—maybe a combination of all three. I sat on a curb. I watched two pigeons humping near a rattlesnake hole while I checked my voice and text messages. No Tigger. It could just be that he was late, but I knew otherwise in the way you just know these things. I started texting all my Jewish friends. "Hey, what are you doing?" "Want to come see a terrible movie—there are six to choose from?" "Anything going on tonight?" But I didn't really want to do anything with any of *them*. The two pigeons were still humping, and I tried to imagine how even a pigeon could be attracted to another pigeon, but then again you could say that about a lot of people.

I took another lap around the lobby, and paced back and forth in front for a few minutes. I was sort of relieved that I didn't have to go through the whole experience of meeting this guy Paul I'd never met before, but disappointed at missing out on the chance to see the Tigger22 with whom I'd become such good friends. If that made sense.

Maybe this was Tigger being sensitive or nervous or something way cute like that. Even so: he'd left me standing here alone in the world's worst theatre. Now we'd have to do the whole What Happened? dance and maybe try this all over again. Or I could just say, "That's that." Before Tigger and I had gotten serious I'd had other online experiences that fizzed out with a no-show (mine, I have to admit). Or some big by-the-way like I Have A Wife And Five Kids. This was the first one that kind of hurt.

My fingers were all greased up. I'd eaten like ten tons of popcorn and there was still three-quarters of the box left. Who decided that people needed THIS much popcorn? Then again, I'd wind up eating the rest because it was there, so even though the popcorn quantity was way out of proportion to people's appetites it still became a self-fulfilling prophecy. And get this: you could get a free refill. So two of them, if you wanted.

I stared at my phone: no messages.

I didn't want to go home and lie to a big house full of people about why I didn't go to the movies. I started walking. Downtown was only about a mile, and that was the direction in which I headed. The hugely loud traffic on Florence Boulevard seemed out of whack with the peaceful golden vista. When you looked beyond all the chain stores and prefab houses, you could imagine horses kicking dust on ancient Saguaros as they galloped across the desert. I walked with the road on my left and rows upon rows of businesses on my right: a drive-up hamburger joint, a discount store, a barber shop, a chain coffee shop, a gas station, a chain pharmacy. If I walked far enough, the stores would start to repeat themselves; there were whole identical *intersections*, spaced a few miles apart,

My sandals rubbed against my big toes. I usually wore band-aids on both big toes because they were always wounded. I'd vacillated a long time between band-aid and no band-aid, trying to conjure the moment when me and Tigger were totally naked. What would be worse: band-aids or two seriously ugly big toes? Tigger didn't have a foot fetish, that much I knew; the guys with foot fetishes let you in on that pretty much first thing.

Besides, being totally naked with a guy, any guy, still seemed a little remote, or ridiculous, or...something. I'd been thinking about sex almost constantly for going-on three years; I owned four vibrating dildos; I'd fantasized about a thousand different guys in a thousand different scenarios; I KNEW this sort of thing happened all the time; yet, it still seemed like something made up. I don't know why I thought that way.

A big-ass SUV honked. The driver, some asshole, was trying to turn right while I was trying to cross to the other side of Florence Boulevard. I pointed at my little white It's Okay To Walk man, and gave the asshole a finger. He rolled down his window, "Merry Christmas to you, too!!!"

This was the first time I'd experienced road rage as a pedestrian. Here was this guy with a seriously oversized, gas-guzzling vehicle that blocked everyone else's view of the road except other seriously oversized vehicles, beeping at me. For walking. With the light. I wanted to crush his Ford Siesta Explorer Champion, or whatever it was called, like a soda can. I didn't, mostly because I was a 98-pound Jewish girl in open-toed, cross-strap, border-stitched leather sandals that hurt like hell. I threw a popcorn kernel at the bumper as the behemoth SUV sped away.

The other side of Florence Boulevard was more of the same: a million uninspiring stores selling a million varieties of useless crap. I arrived at the edge of downtown without really paying attention to anything; it was like I just got there without looking.

Everything was closed. The coffee shop—closed. The Mexican restaurant—closed. The second-hand shop—closed. Christmas window displays were all turned off; Santas, elves and angels hovered in the darkness like prowlers. Even the gas station was closed. I stopped in front of the Paramount Theatre. I sat on the curb with my back to the new marquee. The Paramount opened the year of the Great Depression. At one time, it was totally the best theatre: it had an orchestra pit and big arches and a great balcony and lobby. The original owners didn't survive the Great Depression, and every owner since had fucked it up worse than the owner before. It was closed down for years and years. The new owners vowed to restore it as much as possible to its original condition, but so far the marquee was it.

From the outside, there were remnants of the beautiful Spanish Colonial building of 1929, but you had to look pretty hard and long through all the cracks and scars and bad replastering jobs and layers of paint to see that.

I still had like a quarter of my popcorn left and half the Coke, which was totally watered down because the ice had completely melted.

I stood and walked to the front entrance. Ripped and dusty movie posters were left over from whenever it was the last owners left town. I bet the *Godfather* poster was from when the *Godfather* was a new release. I sipped Coke through my straw. I spit on my palm and wiped a clear spot into the window. I only knew about the theatre's fabulous history from Web sites and newspaper articles; like everything, the great days were long gone by the time I was born. The new owners were in the local paper a lot, mostly over the issue of whether the theatre deserved to be on the National Register of Historic Places. At first, they were turned down, but finally they got accepted.

I looked at the glass cases next to the ticket box—there was an old newspaper clipping for new releases. It was from 1967. Christmas Day, 1967. *The Graduate* and *Guess Who's Coming to Dinner* were the two big Christmas movies; holdover movies from fall and summer were *Bonnie & Clyde*, *The Dirty Dozen*, *To Sir with Love* and *Heat of the Night*.

I walked around to the back of the building. I wanted to see if they'd gotten anywhere with the restoration. The dumpster was filled with trash: crumbled plasterboard, boards with nails sticking out, paint cans, random whatnot. I set my Coke and popcorn on top of an abandoned, rusty old car. I opened the metal trash can lid higher: wasps angrily buzzed and flew about.

The metal back door, I noticed, was ajar. A shaft of light beamed through the darkened crack. I moved toward the door. The alleyway was abandoned except for me and the wasps. I used my gnarly left toe to pry open the door a little more. The theatre was such a big part of downtown, yet it had been closed my whole life. I'd never seen the inside.

A musty smell, like a laundry-load of wet towels, attacked me. Everything was black. A big old ripped projection screen hung from the rafters. I sat where I usually sat when I went to the movies—left aisle seat in the center section, three-quarters of the way back. I sat my Coke on an arm and reached deep in the box for another handful of popcorn. Sitting there, I had a sense of this place in a midlife crisis—halfway between what was and what was going to be. I knew what was had been splendid and hoped what was going to be would be, too, though maybe in an altogether differ- ent way. It made me sad that there was this whole disastrous middle part.

A click echoed through the big, empty theatre. My first thought was, "I'm locked in!!!" Then I heard a nasally, adolescent male voice shriek, "Who's there?" He was nervous, I could tell. Even in the dark I could see it was the most Jewish boy ever. He had dark, springy hair and little wispy sideburns; I would have bet money he was fresh off a Chinese dinner out.

I waved. I guess I was breaking and entering, or at least trespassing, but this didn't feel like a bust. "Hey," he said. "Nobody's supposed to be in here."

"It was open," I said.

He wasn't what you would call good-looking, far from it. He looked *nice*, though, if that makes sense. He was like a Jewish Wally Cleaver. "I ran to get something at the store," he said. "I thought it would be okay to leave it open ten minutes. This door is hard to unlock."

"Learn your lesson?" I asked.

"What are you doing here?"

"I like old theatres."

"Me too," he said. "I clean up this place; when they open again, I'm going to be an usher. Free movies."

He was probably two grades younger than me. He had a really serious posture like you saw with prematurely responsible kids, but his youth ruined that for him. He seemed, all at once, ambitious, kind, smart, and helplessly naïve. He wasn't that bad-looking, really.

"I won't wish you a Merry Christmas," I said.

"Please don't," he said. "I've been getting it all day."

"You're working today?"

"Technically it's once a week, but you can't really do it all in three hours, which is what they want."

"So you're in here for free, doing, like, a better job?"

"I guess so."

I held out my hand. "I'm Dana."

He held his hand well out of my reach and mimicked a shake. "Pleased to meet you; I'm Isaac."

I wasn't sure whether Isaac had cleaning solution on his hand or was afraid of girls, but either way it was charming.

"Are you going to kick me out, Isaac?"

He looked perplexed, like he wouldn't know how to go about such a thing. I was flirting a little. "I don't know; how much longer do you need?"

I tipped my popcorn box toward him, and after some hesitation he dug out two kernels. I extended my Coke, and he sipped from the straw. He had this amazingly cute guilty look, like it was the most preposterously forward thing he'd ever done. He smiled and I smiled, and suddenly I think we both felt like two strangers who'd just kissed in a dark movie theater. It was close.

He started to look around the theatre. In his eyes, I could almost see the room stirring to life. He said, "Want to know something?"

"Yes." I said it in a kind of whisper. He was actually kind of cute.

"What I do when I come here…it's always just me. Except now. After I'm done cleaning I sit in my seat…"

"Which is your seat?"

"Actually? It's the one right next to where you are now."

I hoped he was lying, but I could tell he wouldn't even know how. I patted his seat; he sat.

"I pretend I'm a movie critic…that's what I'm going to do. I'm at a special screening. Every week, it's a new film; I mentally watch the film and take notes for my column."

Not *I want*, but *I'm going to*. I said, "What movies have you not seen?" I don't know why I couldn't stop being a smart ass.

"In a way, I actually do see them. I've pretty much memorized them, so I can play them in my mind almost frame-by-frame. I've seen *Casablanca*, *Citizen Kane*, *North by Northwest* and *The Maltese Falcon*. I've only been doing this a month."

"God, I LOVE those movies," I said. "Humphrey Bogart is probably my favorite all-time actor."

"Did you know that Warner Brothers at first wanted Ronald Reagan and Ann Sheridan to star in *Casablanca*? It was going to be called *Everybody Goes to Rick's*."

"Ronald Reagan, yuck!" I said.

"He wasn't so bad when he was young, but still, he was no Humphrey Bogart. I mean, Bogey's lip scar alone made him perfect. Do you know how he got that lip scar?"

"How?"

"He got it while he was in the Navy. World War II. He was fooling around on the deck…he was a gunner…and he got a splinter. It was the luckiest thing could have happened to him; not only did he get the scar, but it partially paralyzed his lip, thus the lisp."

"Two for the price of one!"

"Exactly."

I'd almost forgotten we were all alone in a mostly-dark old theatre that was once and would be a real treasure. "What's showing today?" I asked.

I could see him blush, even in the dark. "It's stupid, you won't like it."

"Tell!"

"It's a double feature: *Miracle on 34ᵗʰ Street* and *It's a Wonderful Life*."

"Christmas movies? Double Yuck!"

"I don't see them as Christmas movies. They're movies about hope. I know they're really sentimental and all that, but I like them. I like that there were people out there who wanted to make movies that would make everybody feel good. Actually, I love the Marx Brothers for the same reason."

"Do you only like old movies?"

"NO. There are all kinds of great movies from every era; look at *Cider House Rules, Big Night, The Man Who Wasn't There, The Big Lebowski*—anything by the Coen Brothers, really—*Flirting with Disaster, Annie Hall*—all Woody Allen, not including what he did in between *Manhattan Murder Mystery* and *Match Point*...*Match Point* was his comeback film—*Schindler's List, Raging Bull, Blues Brothers, Caddyshack*...there are so many. Old movies are just great in a way you can't do anymore. I like how old movies tell me something about when my mom and dad, or my grandparents, were young. I like how so many things, like computers, hadn't happened yet."

I liked hearing him talk. Isaac: I liked hearing *Isaac* talk. He was actually quite cute, in the way Bogey was very handsome. Despite, no, *because of*, the flaws.

"What's first on the double billing?"

"*It's a Wonderful Life*. I decided to do them chronologically: *It's a Wonderful Life* was released in 1946 and *Miracle on 34th Street* was released in 1947."

"Can I stay and be your movie date? Please: say YES!"

He giggled. We were both staring up and ahead, at the big, dusty, crooked, broken screen. We were developing a rhythm—I dipped for popcorn while his hand hovered on the cusp of the box, he dipped for popcorn while I munched, I sipped the watered-down Coke and passed the drum to my left. I thought briefly about Tigger and the chat room, like something from my past. I couldn't imagine Isaac chatting, not in a million years, much less sending some stranger dick pics or begging for lewd fetish sex.

"Do you have the films memorized?" he asked.

"No. What's the first line from *It's a Wonderful Life*?"

If Isaac didn't know this line, it might have ruined everything. But of course he knew.

"Well, it's Mr. Gower's voice..."

"The drug store owner?"

"Right. He was played by H.B. Warner. H.B. Warner made his first film in 1914. He's been dead nearly 50 years. That's the other thing I like

about old movies—you're not watching celebrities that are on the talk shows every night, you're watching dead people."

"I like that, too."

"You don't see Gower yet. He says, 'I owe everything to George Bailey. Help him, father.' "

He paused, and I snuck a look at him concentrating there in the dark. "I should back up. FADE IN: it's a night sequence. You see various shots of Bedford Falls, a small town in upstate New York. Streets are deserted. Snow is falling. It's Christmas Eve. Now, over the scenes of Bedford Falls, you hear Gower's voice praying…"

I jumped in, *"I owe everything to George Bailey. Help him, father."*

We both giggled, and I wished I could redeem my free popcorn refill: I knew we would be there for the whole show.

Family Update

Stewart punched the radio station button. "You don't like Elton John, do you?" I did, or at least I'd been enjoying that song.

"Put on whatever you want," I responded.

Big skies spanned miles upon miles ahead and behind, little white curlicued clouds painted into somber blue. We'd had an exceptionally warm winter. Snow covered the mountains, but at lower altitudes the landscape was bare, wet and pliable. The Range Rover's snow chains barreled along 89, and clunked over potholes as we passed through Gardiner and then Yellowstone's north entrance. It looked like rain. I said, "It looks like rain, Stew."

"Not a chance," he said. "I checked all the reliable forecasts before we left. It won't rain all weekend, and it's too warm for snow. The dew point..." My attention drifted. Stew, like my sister Katie, his wife, never knew when to stop. Big talkers, both of them.

Stew belonged to the Sierra Club and taught plant identification classes part time; he even led a boy scout troop, though he didn't have kids. He was a birder, a hiker, and a rock climber. All that aside, it was going to rain. The sky had that Fuck You gray tint to it, and the air through my cracked window smelled metallic. "I'm pretty sure it's going to rain," I said.

"Nonsense," he said, with his characteristic smugness. "You leave all the planning and details to me. I am Class-A certified…"

The Family Update had arrived, as usual, on the second business day after Thanksgiving. For me, this marked the start of the holiday season, when dormant animosity, more so even than good will, revived. The whole family hated Stewart. He rubbed us the wrong way, and then compounded problems with what seemed an almost deliberate obliviousness to our irritation. We tolerated him in person, but in closed sessions it was a verbal lynch mob. Mom would start, "Well, he had another fit because Shelly threw up on his precious Oriental carpet. He wants to get rid of her."

"Oh listen to this," Frank would say.

I had just finished *The Year-In-Review* and was launching into *Kudos*, when the phone rang. It was my sister Katie. "Hi Donald."

"I got the Update."

"Don't make fun. Stewart worked *so* hard on that."

For Katie, our dislike of Stewart had become a sensitive subject. At first, she hadn't noticed. Then she noticed. Now, Katie's mission was for Stewart to gain acceptance, perhaps even love.

"No, it's good."

"Actually, that's why I called."

Immediately, I didn't like the sound of it. And I was right. "I'm going to ask you for a huge favor, Donald, and you can't say no. Okay, I know everybody has issues with Stewart, so you don't have to pretend everybody doesn't have issues with Stewart." *Issues* was a word Katie had gotten from Stewart. At least she hadn't said *problematic* or *dialogic*. "The thing is, I think if you showed everybody you actually liked Stewart, and if Stewart actually thought you liked him, things would be different. Everybody looks up to you. You're, like, the family's idea of successful, plus, aren't you, like, the King of Christmas Gifts? I mean, you're always coming up with these way interesting…"

I stopped her, because Katie wasn't inclined to stop herself. "I don't not like Stewart." It was the strongest polite statement I could think of on the spot.

"It doesn't have to be off that list, I know you hate lists." The Update, it seemed to me, was an elaborate ruse to publish Stew and Katie's personal Christmas lists. "But something…good. Something *perfect*. It's got to be the *perfect* Christmas present. You know what I mean? You know, forget the list and just go after it. Like that one time you got…"

Katie continued to talk and I sort of listened, until, finally, she came to what I understood to be the point. "I don't care what it is, just that it's the kind of gift he opens and everybody's like Wow!"

"*Wow?*"

"Exactly."

Going camping in Yellowstone Park had been my idea; doing it the weekend before Christmas had been Stew's. He had papers to grade, and a faculty Christmas party, this and that, which left this last weekend as the only weekend we could do it. When I tried to back out, when I said, "It was just an idea," Stew came up with a million ways to make it work, such that I sensed he really wanted this.

I saw the weekend as a brothers-in-law getting to know one another trip. Ice fishing, hiking, stories around the campfire: those sorts of tried-and-true bonding activities. Maybe I'd discover whatever it was Katie loved about Stew, some insight into him as a likeable, caring, decent person, and in doing so get clever gift ideas out of the weekend.

Speed limit signs of 45 miles per hour were posted along the lonely two-lane road into the park, along with cautions about wildlife and other potential hazards. We penetrated deeper into the interior. The vast, abandoned national park emitted an aura of serenity, and, maybe because of the clouds, looming disaster. Stew tramped all over the serenity with neurotic station flipping. Against the backdrop of a ratty asphalt road winding ever toward an evil horizon, we heard, zzzzzzt. "In entertainment…" Ppppppphhhhhhhhhttttt. "Come and get your…." Sssshhhooop.

"Baby..." zzzzzzt. There were no other cars. Only hardcore campers came out in December, much less this close to Christmas, and I wondered now if it was purely a comfort issue, or if safety were a factor.

"Do we know where we're going?" I asked.

"You *don't* know where we're going; I *do* know where we're going," he said. That, right there. It was not only what he said, but how he said it. He felt superior to us, and I think he thought we agreed.

Stew and I were both teachers, but he taught at the college level and I taught high school. We shared a lot of the same day-to-day challenges. But he dismissed what I did, even once, in his condescending way, guessing that my biggest challenge was "Refereeing." I taught an elective journalism class and physical education, and ran the school newspaper and varsity baseball team. I'd poured 12 years into that high school, and was proud of my work. Stewart was a junior professor in the English Department at MSU; he taught courses such as Introduction to Language, Survey of Literary Criticism, Literature of the American Indian, and Images of Women in Literature and the Arts.

By the time Stew parked the car in an isolated "pullout" near a running stream, we'd put an hour and a half between us and the entrance at which we'd paid our camping fee. We exited the car. We heard the echoing squawk of a great big scavenger bird. A sign warned, "Not a designated camp ground."

"We can't stay here overnight," I said.

"These rules are tourist season stuff," Stew assured me. "If somebody were to come by—and they won't—we'll pack up and move. But they won't."

Stew ordered me to relax while he set up camp. "Stew, I was a boy scout, too..."

He waved me off, as if I were a dear, spirited old invalid. The wind made a big ruckus: dead leaves lifted up and fell down; twigs snapped; my coat rustled; the car antennae bobbed. It was cold. As Stewart constructed the tent, I ignited the aluminum camp stove. I'd assembled a hot chocolate kit back home, and I now silently congratulated myself on such foresight. I began to enjoy myself. I sat in a folding chair and manned the pot like a scavenger after the hunt. I added chocolate chunks to the melting brew, splashed in milk and sugar, and stirred the liquid with a stick. I sprinkled cinnamon over the top.

Stew, between trips to and from the car, stopped. He grabbed the stick from me. "No," he said. He launched into a lecture about the chemical properties of chocolate that lasted a good six minutes, by which time he'd saved the hot chocolate from sure ruin and distributed the liquid in exact measurements throughout four plastic canteens.

I dumbly drank. I hadn't camped a lot, and not in a long time, but I had common sense. The hot chocolate suddenly lost its appeal.

"Let me help, Stew; I want to help," I said.

He pooh-poohed me with a wave of his hand. I watched Stew work; that was all there was for me now. He went 6-foot and a little, but there was no way to think of him as big. He was scrawny, pale, and collegiate. His plaid, high-end hiking clothes weighed more than his stick figure body, and his posture cried, "Look at me! I'm important!!" He was one of those academics who hated academics, always charging his colleagues with being out of touch with "the real world," when, in fact, Stewart had gone straight from high school to college to graduate school to university faculty. He'd never seen the inside of an office building, much less a warehouse.

"Chow's ready," Stew announced. Words like *chow* were, in Stew's mind, what connected him to the common man and distanced him from the academics. We ate. It was amazing to watch Stewart eat pork beans and hot dogs and slurp water without ever once slowing down his lecture on The Outdoors. Night had fallen. A chain of bright dots wound through the storm sky. A thousand little wilderness noises electrified our makeshift camp. Tired from travel, we sprawled out along the embankment. Were we bonding? Was I finally gaining insight into the qualities that endeared Stew to my sister? It was hard to say, because Stewart was midway through a 14-minute lecture on the merits of quiet.

"Told you it wasn't going to rain," Stew announced, through the dark. Stew was the kind of person, he made you root for rain. I'd take the soggy socks. I'd take the sloshy hiking boots. Give me the second-degree pneumonia. It would all be worth it to say, "I told YOU."

"I'll try not to wake you in the morning," Stew promised. "I'm up before dawn. I have an unnatural store of energy. Genetically speaking…" And so on. Stew blew out our torch lights, and then I heard his footsteps crunch toward his tent. Inside my own little tent, I burned a kerosene lamp as the stream swished and owls hooted. I unpacked my backpack. Though the temperature had dropped to near freezing, Stew had set up a propane contraption that blew hot air into the tent. It was snug. Sitting in my collapsible director's chair, I wondered why Stew had wanted this trip, or if I'd misread his signals. He seemed casually annoyed at the world's incompetence, represented, at the moment, by me.

I read and reread the Update. Stew's *Wish List* began, as always, with a philosophical statement on the meaning of gift exchange, then a summary of how his new list reflected growth and change that had transpired over the course of a meaningful year. He organized his list, like a newspaper, into six distinct categories—*Fashion, Entertainment, Home, The Arts, Sport,* and—my favorite—*Knowledge.* Under each subheading were bullet points with careful labels and descriptions.

For example. Under *Knowledge,* he wrote, "Having privately undertaken the study of contemporary British literature this past year, I am naturally interested in obtaining prime novels for my collection. First, a definition of *contemporary.* While some scholars equate *contemporary* with *living,* for my purposes I will select 1950 as the somewhat arbitrary starting point. This naturally allows us to include the vast body of work by authors such as Graham Greene, Virginia Wolff, Somerset Maugham, P.G. Wodehouse (I do so enjoy a good chuckle now and again), and Salmon Rushdie (yes, he's *English*). This Christmas, unlike past Christmases, I will be seeking only cloth or leather-bound first editions. Bindings should be tight. Check carefully for bumps and discoloration. Original dust jackets, definitely. Please, please NO Book Club reprints or library discards. Absolutely NO paperbacks."

Wind whispered outside my tent. My kerosene lamp's flame faded. A tree branch scuffled against the canvas, such that it sounded like a small burrowing animal.

My own philosophy of gift exchange was that a gift should be a revelation. It should be something the gift receiver knew he must have only at the instant he unwrapped it. There should be synergy between the giver and receiver, and the gift should acknowledge, even enhance, some shared passion. I hated lists. If we were all going to buy pre-selected gifts off each other's lists, we might as well agree on a dollar figure and do our own shopping.

I woke the next morning to lumbering, clumsy shuffling sounds. I thought: bear. I hurriedly dressed, and grabbed a stick. Dawn was breaking. It was rosy and cold and the air felt completely white. Holding my stick in a ludicrous crouch, I stared into the thick underbrush. Young naked Aspens bent at the knees of old, furry pines. I meant to scare off the bear, though I was more than a little nervous. What if the bear looked at me, looked at himself, and was pretty good at calculating odds? A symphony of crackles and whirls and wisps and chirps and caws sallied forth from the great, mysterious, noble forest. It rapidly grew lighter. The source of the lumbering, clumsy shuffling sounds had disappeared, and so, tension draining from my body, I started my day.

The next two and a half hours were glorious. I washed dirty dishes in the stream. I gathered kindling on a leisurely stroll through the forest. I made comfortable log and stone furniture—two chairs, little end tables, and a dining table. I canvassed the dewy ground for worms and bugs, used the bait to catch two nice trout. I cleaned and filleted the fish, started a fire and, dipping into Stew's supply cooler, started breakfast. With the fire roaring, I fried fish, sautéed mushrooms, scrambled some eggs. I sliced up tomatoes. I heated the coffee.

Then Stewart awoke.

He scampered about the camp, all the while explaining how very exceptional it was he had slept until late morning and citing evidence, anecdotal and statistical, supporting his legendary energy. He went through the kindling, tossing stick after stick off to the side; added salt and pepper to the scrambled eggs; rejected several clean forks and cups; splashed the entire pot of coffee into the grass and started another pot; rearranged end tables and chairs. He never, ever stopped talking. Finally, he planted his pencil legs wide apart, put his hands on his hips, and surveyed the camp. He had the look of somebody who'd just fixed an almost unfixable problem. "There," he said. "Now let me serve you some breakfast."

He seized control of the food I'd prepared. After a bit, I was sitting in my chair like a drooling, helpless child while Stewart condescended to feed me.

"Did you just get up?" Stewart asked. That. It was the kind of casual, insensitive remark that incensed the family. Not that I needed congratulations, but it seemed deliberately mean-spirited for Stew to undervalue my work. Or maybe it wasn't deliberate, which might have been worse.

"I guess I've been up close to three hours," I said. "A bear woke me."

Stew started laughing maniacally. He literally slapped his knee with his hand. He wore this smarmy grin that said, "Oh, how delicious."

"What's so funny, Stew?"

"You've been watching too much *Yogi Bear*. There aren't any bears *here*. Not in December. Bears, all wildlife, in fact, gravitate toward warm thermal areas…" The next 19 and a half minutes were devoted to a lesson about Yellowstone National wildlife, mostly the habits of grizzly and black bears. Stew informed me that Grizzly, or Brown, Bears, moved to higher altitudes and hibernated in dens for up to six months. Black Bears, similarly, were asleep. "Food is scarce…" Stew, like Katie, would rather forfeit a toe than the podium. His lips kept flapping, flapping, flapping. It baffled me how two talkers like that ever came to know one another. They must have had exhausting conversations over coffee during their courtship, each trying to wedge and ram and slice their way into the conversation, and then, having succeeded, mightily trying to hold serve. I would think the big talkers would troll for big listeners, and vice versa, but that wasn't the case here.

"To even think we'd see a bear in the northwestern edge of Yellowstone National Park, in December, you'd have to know almost literally nothing about bears." I was now rooting for a team of murderous black bears to invade our camp during a monsoon.

We hiked after breakfast. I reminded myself, "If Katie can take it full time, I can at least put in a few part-time shifts now and then." I focused on The Perfect Gift. Stew rambled on about this and that, segued from one long, only slightly relevant soliloquy to another long, only slightly relevant soliloquy. Despite Stew's prodigious output of words, I gained little or no insight into either his worth or motivation as a fellow human being. Stew walked slightly ahead, carrying a stick he used to slap at underbrush that didn't need to be slapped at. It was refreshingly cold. White, along with a touch of blue, infused the gray sky. The air still held that metallic storm feel, though, and I was still sure it would rain.

Stew nattered on about bulletin board wars in his department. No kidding: the various professors and assistant professors fought over space, and apparently Stew himself had written a scathing six-page "memo" thoroughly promoting the importance of literary theorists over creative writers. We covered two, almost three miles before this diatribe lost its steam, and then I made the mistake of asking, "Who gives a shit?" which promoted a considered analysis of the power politics at play in the controversy. That got us back to the camp.

Stew ordered me to "take a load off" while he dicked around. Night fell. A strong breeze blew out our torchlights, and after several failed attempts to relight them we just let it be dark. Stew shifted his chair. He tapped his leather-top Bean Boots against the hard ground. Gusts of wind overpowered all the other little night sounds, except that scuffling sound from this morning. I thought, "Come on, rain!" I prayed, "Have at us, bear!!"

I decided to test a theory. It had occurred to me that Stewart didn't listen to or care about anybody else. "Stew," I started. "Daniel's very self-conscious about being tall. He skies over the other kids his age. I'm trying to make him understand that nature will take its due course. How tall were you at his age?"

"What is he, nine?" Daniel was six, which made Stew's guess 50 percent too heavy. We went on like this. He didn't know my daughter had worn braces the past year and a half. He didn't know my wife held masters degrees in both English and History. He didn't know my varsity had won the conference title four straight years. But ask him what toothpaste brand he preferred and he had a 20-minute prepared hunk on scientific studies that debunked fluoride as a cavity fighter, as well as an aside on current thought in the dental community vis-à-vis the brushing sideways versus up-and-down debate.

Inside my tent, I felt this incredible gratitude to be left alone. So, what did I actually know about Stewart? I went to my backpack. My wife had saved all the previous Family Updates, and now I reviewed the four-volume set. Katie and Stewart had been married in the summer of 1999. The Family Updates revealed a certain rise in socio-economic status, and a movement toward middle class comfort. In the first update, Stewart and Katie rented a low-end apartment on the outskirts of the university. Subsequently, they got a higher-end apartment in the heart of the university district, and now they'd purchased a starter home "off campus." There had been promotions with their associated pay raises, and silly academic awards. There was an ever-changing roster of pets: a couple of parakeets, a cat, then another cat, a dog they got at the animal shelter, then subtract the dog, who "had to be put down," a hamster. Stewart won third place in some apparently prestigious bridge tournament. Katie's high school friend (well, somebody she knew but not well enough to keep in touch with after graduation) died in a car wreck. Stewart's father was diagnosed with skin cancer, but had beaten it by the following Christmas. I noticed that the heading *Knowledge* was a revision of the original heading, *Learning*.

What did this say about the Stewart's true character? What insight did I have into Stewart's hopes and dreams? How did Stewart see himself, and in his toughest, darkest moments of self-revelation, what flaws scared him most?

I couldn't answer these questions. Being with Stew made me understand less, not more. Is it right to assume everybody has a good side? Can we honestly say all people, given the proper chance and context, will eventually demonstrate a compassionate nature? Or are some people as they seem, selfish and spiteful and ill-humored?

I slept fitfully that night, dreaming, literally, of home. On our last morning, a Sunday, I again woke hours before Stew. The campsite was torn apart. Garbage (it was a carry in-carry out policy) trailed from our car to the edge of the tree line. The wood pile was scattered. A trail of faint paw prints led to and from our campsite. Bear?

The dawn sky held a menacing blackness. As I sipped my morning coffee, so looking forward to the end of the weekend, I hoped rain would redeem me. I hoped the bear would return. Seven cups of coffee later, Stew's tent rustled. He yawned, "This is really, really strange, I never—I mean *never*—sleep past dawn, it must be something..." Who knew a yawn could stretch the length of a theory on the effects of the forest on human inner chronometers. Stew finally saw the camp, which I'd left in the condition I'd found it. "A raccoon must have gotten into our stuff," he said.

"Look at the prints," I said. "Too big for a raccoon."

He stooped down. He tilted his head sideways. He scooped up dirt and sniffed it, as if applying some conclusive field testing method. "Raccoon," he said, with finality. "These prints just appear bigger..."

I stopped him. "It's not a fucking raccoon," I said.

It slipped out that way. Just like that, Stew, whether he chose to acknowledge it or not, knew I had *issues*. He started talking. He kept talking. It was a lot of nonsense designed to prove, beyond a shadow of a doubt, that Stew was right and everybody else, me especially, was wrong. I stood. I picked up Stew's walking stick. I shoved it into his gut and said, "Come on, we're going bear hunting."

We tramped through the forest. I did not say a word. Stew did not, for lack of oxygen, say a word. I kept up an aggressive, anaerobic pace that had us sweating beneath our Gortex vests. I didn't really know anything about bears, much less how to track one, and I wasn't sure what I was hoping to accomplish. I picked up more faint tracks and followed them. I took us deeper into the forest. Maybe I just wanted to humble Stew, or perhaps, in my own way, scream out my anger. Stew tried several times to slow the pace. He bent forward and gasped. I was, despite being six years his senior, in ten times better shape than Stew, and I punished him with determined uphill climbs and rapid descents.

It was hard to tell the rain had started. We heard it trickling through the trees long before we felt it. The treetops, so high in the sky, received the first cold, December drops minutes before the water cascaded to our level. Branches sagged beneath the water weight, but at the same time greenery around us seemed to ping. The moment our wool caps began

to absorb the moisture, I realized I had no idea where we were, and as I glanced at Stew doubled over in pain I half rooted for him to know the way back and half rooted for him to be lost, as well.

I stopped. I'd focused the whole time on bear, not landscape. Every direction looked approximately like the direction in which we'd started. The woods were dark as night. The leafy ground covering was soft, slick and soggy. Tall, narrow tree trunks surrounded us, like prison bars. Stew stood huddled over himself, winded and wet and, it seemed from my angle, entirely sad. In my anger, I'd left my mobile phone back at the car, which now seemed like a completely irresponsible thing to have done. "Stew, I have to admit: I'm lost."

Stew raised his body. He looked around. "Me, too," he said.

The process of finding, securing, and ultimately presenting a gift should be a difficult, nearly impossible journey, and result, ultimately, in that gift finding a place equally in the hearts of both giver and receiver. You have to not want to give it up. The idea, I think, is to embellish, if not complete, some tiny hidden part of a person's life.

Stew and I, two old boy scouts, were finally on such a journey. Hiking in the woods seemed like a fairly straightforward, common experience—people did it all the time. But get lost in an impossibly big national park in December, when no other people are out, and you're in trouble.

I turned from one possible route home to another to another, tiny music box turns. When I completed the circle, I did it again. Stewart also turned and turned. Our rotating bodies orbited each other. The rain kept falling: dirt turned to a hard mud, dead leaves turned deeper shades of brown and red, we got wetter and wetter. Whatever animal tracks there might have been were washed away, along with our own footprints.

Stew's teeth chattered and his mouth turned blue, but, surprisingly, he kept his wits. "Okay," he said. He was clearly in pain. "I don't know which direction is which. I should have brought my compass; I usually bring my compass. Let's try to remember a few landmarks between here and the car."

"Good idea," I said. It was the first conversation we'd ever had in which we were equal partners. "The last marker I remember...do you remember the tree with graffiti on it?"

"Hansel was here!"

"Gretel, too," I recalled the punch line. I paused. "Sorry about this bear chase, Stew."

He waved his hand, like, "Forget about it." He said, "We find that tree, we're back on the trail. That's where we broke off. I know I can get us back from there."

"Okay, that tree was no more than an hour from here. Do you have a watch?" Stew nodded. "Take a guess. Which way do you think?" He pointed. "Okay, if we don't see the tree in an hour, we turn back and come to this spot. Then we try another direction."

We walked the hour, then to be sure we walked another 15 minutes. We concluded it was the wrong way, and hiked back. Stew gasped for breath. "Are you okay, Stew?" Rain fell harder. Drops did not so much fall through the trees as pour off the leaves. If we rested, Stew got wetter; if we continued, Stew got more fatigued. "I can make it."

I took Stew's backpack, and we tried the next direction: same results. The next: same. Each round trip took two and a half hours; more, actually, since Stew's pace had slowed considerably, and the rain seeped deep into our marrow. He was in bad shape. He coughed these jagged, wet coughs, and wrapped his arms around himself for warmth. "There's only one more way, Stew."

"I have to rest." He slumped to the ground. Puddles formed in ruts and holes, and I watched water flow downhill. "The stream," I exclaimed. "Is that *our* stream?" We watched the water slowly trickle down and to the right, which was not the last way to the tree. Our camp was downstream or upstream, one way or the nother. The graffiti tree? I was confused. I looked at Stew. He sat holding his muddy boots with limp, shivering fingers, bent over as if to hide from the elements. Little sobs punctuated the jagged cough.

I did not, could not, think we were no closer to the solution. I had started to feel the chill, and now that we'd stopped my muscles grew tired. Darkness covered the entire forest. The temperature dipped dramatically.

I checked my pocket watch: eight o'clock, or nearly twelve hours lost in the forest.

"We have to try the last way," I said.

Stew was completely silent. I helped him to his feet. He dragged his body forward. We did the hour-long trek in about two. No tree. How could that be? We'd both seen the graffiti tree—there was definitely a graffiti tree—and we'd systematically gone in each possible direction. Had we underestimated the distance? Was the graffiti tree somewhere between one and another path we'd hiked? Was it possible we could have missed the graffiti tree?

Stew slumped down again, catatonic. He needed to get dry, to get warm, to get medical attention. But to hurry when you're lost is just to rapidly change starting points. We hiked back toward the stream. After several minutes, we came to a little cave. We had no idea where we were in relation to the car. We entered the cave. It was dark and damp and smelled of Earth the way you'd imagine Earth pre-Industrial Revolution. I yelled into the cave, "Hell-o, Hell-o." Whatever lived in there, I wanted to encourage to fly out now. There were little, unidentifiable noises resonating throughout the depths of the cave, and so Stew and I hiked just far enough from the mouth to get away from the rain and wind. I had matches, protected by plastic baggie, in my pocket. My eyes adjusted a little and I found a paper bag, and a couple of sticks. All dry enough. I needed to get a serious fire going, though; I left Stew and went out gathering small, wet kindling.

The little fire created enough heat to roast the wetter kindling. I made a stand in order to suspend the wet kindling over the heat—now *this* was camping—but it wasn't sturdy, and so I had to hold it myself. The fire took all my energy. As long as I manned the fire, we could not think about finding our way back; if I didn't man the fire, we might freeze.

Stew slept. I hoped that was good. While he dozed, I riffled through his backpack and found energy bars, two apples, a small jar of peanut butter, bread and juice boxes. Our clothes dried out some. I could see my breath in big, billowing spirals, a rich exhalation one part deep freeze and two parts campfire smoke.

We passed the night of December 23, and then all of Christmas Eve, like this. I stepped out of the cave at regular intervals, and twice heard what sounded like faraway barks and sirens. But any search party would naturally look at designated camp grounds, so even our car, much less ourselves, would be hard to locate. I slept in tiny increments, aware that it was up to me to keep the fire alive. I sweated. I stripped down to my t-shirt, and dried my other clothes, piece by piece; I did the same for Stew. I'd been such as ass, letting vanity or some obscure sense of pride lead me into a wild, dangerous bear chase. This, most of all, was what we all hated about Stewart: he brought out the worst in us.

We revived. Our clothes were dry, we were well fed and hydrated, rested.

"Merry Christmas," I said.

"You, too," Stewart said.

"We're going to be okay," I said. "You ever see *Grizzly Adams*, the movie?

Stewart nodded.

"He lived in the woods all the time. We just have to make it until tourist season."

Stewart laughed. He said, "You're supposed to stay put, that's the conventional wisdom."

"Not in a cave, I'll bet."

"No."

"Let's find a road, our car, the hiking trail, something. You okay to go?"

"Yeah."

That sequence of unadorned answers—the nod, *no*, and *yes*—told me that Stew was either humbled or sicker even than he seemed. We stepped out of the cave. The sun glared high above us. The ground was soft, but dry.

"We have to be able to find the cave again, in case," he said.

"The barks and sirens were…that way," I said, pointing. "That must be the way to the road."

We set off at an ambling pace, not saying much. I wasn't, for some reason, worried. I felt as one does after having passed a difficult test, though I guess I should have felt as one does in the midst of a difficult test. I thought. I thought about the fact that I honestly didn't like Stew, and that if this weekend hadn't changed that nothing likely would. I also thought about how that was okay: I loved Katie enough to put up with him.

Shortly, we came to a clearing on the horizon. We marched toward it. A misty yellow pallor hung over a faded green field; mountains were all around. We distinctly heard human voices. I knew immediately, like a base hit to break open a close game, that our ordeal was over. Stew, then I, tentatively stepped toward the voices; several tourists and hikers acknowledged our presence with friendly nods of their heads. All eyes were fixed on an idle geyser in the center of the field. Stew and I, almost in step, approached a couple seated on a nearby bench.

"You never know when this one will go off, but they think soon," the woman said.

We wanted only to return to safety. But when we explained our predicament to the couple, the man said, "Be happy to take you somewhere, after she goes."

Stew launched into a six-minute lecture about various stress conditions, then parlayed that with a four-minute piece on respiratory illnesses, at which point the woman steeled up and said, "Like my husband said, we'd be happy to give you a lift…AFTER she goes."

I sat on the nearest bench. We were silent. Stewart stared at the idle geyser; I stared at the idle geyser. The couple stared at the idle geyser. It was a silvery, twinkling morning; resilient with a crisp air that made my lungs feel younger. The old couple looked determined to see what they came to see, or maybe they were just putting Stewart in his place. I thought about my wife, my kids, Katie, and tried to borrow a cell phone from a lone hiker. "No signal," he said. "I just tried." Stew was nodding off. I thought maybe I needed to better define the word "rescue" to the old couple, but I held my tongue.

I waited. I thought about how there could be no good gift for somebody you didn't like, and that was what made Christmas and all phony holidays like Valentine's Day such shams: all the shitty gifts you felt duty-bound to bestow upon co-workers, clients, disapproving mothers-in-law, abusive fathers, crank brothers-in-law, lovers for whom you harbored serious doubt, even mediocre postmen. Children, of course, relished their presents, but even there expectation often overshadowed anticipation. I waited some more. I waited and waited. But there was also this magical side to holidays, too, that moment when the ideal giver found that perfect present for the ideal receiver.

Here I was, exhausted but also delirious, about to deliver Stewart to a worried, helpless family on Christmas Day. Even Stew's biggest detractors, like my mother, would surely feel a surge of joy upon seeing him safe. She might even happily listen to his babbling with something like joy, for at least this one Christmas day.

I stared at the silent geyser. It seemed, at the moment, so common, but we all knew it had the potential to thrill. That it was *going to* thrill. I waited for the awe-inspiring natural wonder to do its thing, so I, and Stew, could finally get home.

Bah!

The gargantuan black gate sealed off the dark courtyard. Cheerless tar-stained buildings blocked out the sparkling Lanesboro, Minnesota, dawn. I lifted the heavy Marley's Head knocker, dropped it against thick treated wood. The bang ricocheted around my soft brain tissues. I dropped it again. A third time.

"Why, bless my soul, who is that?"

Everything sounded, that morning, like clanging symbols. My immediate reaction to human voice was, "Ssssh." But my boss, Albert Wigley, insisted we get into character even before customers arrived. Wigley was a frustrated stage actor. As a youth, he'd chased the dream—stock theatre companies, bit parts in big productions, big parts in bit productions, call backs for big parts in big productions, the occasional hair rinse commercial. He was good enough and lucky enough to always be encouraged, but not good enough or lucky enough to ever get what he was after. His was a face that screamed character actor: a bulbous red nose, a lazy right eye, reedy lips set against a dimpled chin. Wigley always seemed to be looking somewhere else, or in two other places, while ostensibly looking at you.

"'Tis I, Ebenezer Scrooge." I said.

The gigantic door creaked open. "My dear sir, come in out of the cold," Wigley replied, seemingly looking at a stone Oliver Twist fountain in the courtyard's farthest most corner. I carried my costume in a dry cleaner bag, my shoes and accessories in a duffel bag. I wore brown corduroy pants and an untucked white shirt, with my Wayfarer glasses settled on my head. "Thank'ee for your munificence, Sir."

A wooden ladder leaned against one of the courtyard's dozen unlit gas lamps. Warren Wigley, a 12-year-old with his father's unfortunate bulbous nose, practiced for his role as lamplighter. He wore deliberately scruffy, oversized corduroys with suspenders and a sweater—*jumper*, sorry—and a scarf that began at his neck and wrapped around him all the way to his stomach. His scrunched-up face was dabbed with rouge and kohl powder and snot, giving the dour child a sooty, rosy appearance halfway between abandoned and pampered. A folly thermometer read 15 below zero on a crisp but sunny day I suspected would reach the low 40s. Mrs. Wigley, aka The Niece By Marriage, applied the final squirts of snow paint to the window rims. Folly icicles hung from the barnyard lawn ornaments. Holly sprigs and berries brightened the windows.

The Wigleys, who'd met and married in their middle ages, used inheritance money to establish this homage to Dickens. The Old Curiosity Bed and Breakfast enabled them both—Mrs. Wigley was a former aspiring model whose winning looks were buried beneath waves of quivering fat, wrinkles, and a bad tan job—to regain the stage. Wigley grabbed me by the shoulders. "My young apprentice, you must concentrate, you must focus, you must see, feel, you must *be* your character," he said, while seeming to check out the woodpile near the shed. He shouted and gestured with a saliva-soaked flourish. "Keep this illuminated thought in your head: the part of Scrooge is really a dual role. After the epiphany, which is to say sometime after dessert, Scrooge becomes Reformed Scrooge. You've got to sell two and a half acts of Bah Humbug to *earn* that ending."

Wigley's 9 a.m. energy level annoyed, no *pained*, me. It hurt just to stand there. Knowing Christmas Day would be sacrificed to this, I'd overdone Christmas Eve. It had started innocently enough but ended at a sticky kitchen table with sucked limes, spilled salt and a bottle of Jose Lopez. I thought, as Wigley went on and on about how knowing your lines did *not* mean knowing your character, that it only lasted one day. One dry Christmas, and I would wake tomorrow to a clean bill of health.

"You have to play Scrooge as *a squeezing, wrenching, grasping, scraping, clutching, covetous old sinner!*" Wigley screamed, his stare fixed, at once, on the humble Christmas tree in the center of the courtyard and a pigeon alighting near the chimney. "You must *edge your way along the crowded paths of life, warning all human sympathy to keep its distance.*"

Wigley might as well have played *I'll Be Home for Christmas* with a ball peen hammer to the side of my head. I'd gulped prodigious amounts of water before bed and upon rising, taken Vitamin E supplements, popped extra-strength aspirin. I even did ten vigorous minutes on the exercise bike to sweat some of it out. Nothing helped. This was a hangover that had me trapped in a dark alleyway with no exit.

Wigley would play Scrooge's nephew Fred. He was in his mid-50s and broad around the middle, slightly crumpled, whereas the Nephew of *A Christmas Carol* was 30ish, fit, energetic, handsome and wholesome. Clearly a poor casting choice. But it was Wigley's B & B, so that made him the producer, director, casting director, set designer, lighting crew and, yes, noble, kind, optimistic Fred.

"Bah, off with you now," I said, and headed toward the changing room.

"A merry Christmas, uncle, God save you!" trailed after me.

The sprawling, echoing estate felt utterly spooky. Though many of the buildings and rooms had been converted to various uses, there were still buildings and rooms that existed as abandoned shells. The idea was to convert all the damp, corroded, musky-smelling rooms into bright, fixed-up, cinnamon-smelling guest rooms. But it was a one-at-a-time effort.

I stepped through a crumbling corridor into a makeshift dressing room. I desperately wanted the throbbing to stop. I popped two Advil and washed them down with more water. I stood perfectly still a second, two, and it dawned on me that actually, in fact, I felt pretty okay. Wait: *not* pretty okay.

Our little community catered to tourists. Spring, summer and fall people came to bike and hike along the Root River Trail, or else canoe in the river itself. Winters were the dead time, but the quaint factor—coffee shops, b & b's, places that sold kitty-shaped teapots—was strong enough to keep a steady flow of visitors.

Guests would start arriving just before noon. These would be happy, spirited, grateful people, and not just that, but happy, spirited, grateful people with cameras. Nothing hurts a hangover worse than a fake smile.

I decided, then, that today would be my last day. I'd tried in vain to quit a half-dozen times over the past year, but Wigley, who saw me as his star protégé, wouldn't hear of it. I gave official notice twice. Or, actually, I said, "I've thought it over, and as soon as you can find a replacement…I need a change, and as much as it kills me…you've been so great and Mrs. W's been so great…I need to leave here as soon as you can find a replacement…I'll of course stay until you find a replacement." He kept putting me on the schedule, and even once drove over to my place to get me when I'd decided to just not go in.

I thought I would move to Minneapolis, which offered not only more opportunities but anonymity. Deep down, I wanted out of acting. I wanted a respectable, middle-class job with an office and a parking space. But I'd pinned all my youthful hopes on Becoming An Actor, advertised my imminent success to friends and relatives and people I met on the bus or at parties. The stagnation I called a career embarrassed me more and more as the years passed. I feared I would become Wigley. More so, I feared I'd become Wigley without the inheritance. Yet, I could not clearly foresee how to reroute from this dead end course. Wigley lived vicariously through me, and at times I wanted to believe I was special enough to rise above the thousands and thousands just like me. *Exactly* like me. As long as I had this job, I held onto that tiny hope; as long as I had this job, I would not have to face up to the task of disappointing Wigley; as long as I had this job I could bluff my way through awkward conversations with friends and relatives and people I met on the bus or at parties.

As long as had this job, I would never get that respectable job.

"It's a bad time; we can't replace you right now," Wigley always pleaded.

Hangovers give you perspective. Standing in front of a streaked, crooked mirror, looking at my streaked, crooked reflection, I realized, "Look at me!" I could not, would not, go on indefinitely dressing like Ebenezer Scrooge whilst serving English professor-wannabees duck. Maybe it was impossible to resign, but I could almost certainly get myself fired. I *would* get myself fired.

The gruff old clock sounded eleven chimes. By now, the entire staff had arrived. Mrs. Wigley fluttered into Pip Hall, like a diva taking the stage. She clapped her hands thrice. We ceased fluffing flowers, stopped shining silverware, postponed primping place mats. Conversation grinded, then halted. "Allow me, gentlemen, to make a preamble to this, our most festive day of the season here at Old Curiosity."

It was amazing to witness the sheer volume of base cream up close. It was like really, really studying the paint swirls on the ceiling and realizing it wasn't all solid eggshell, that there was a pattern. Everything about Mrs. Wigley was false—her hair color, her eyelashes, her eye color, the whiteness of her teeth, the tan of her skin. Her breasts, obviously. And, of course, her accent.

"Thank'ee, one and all, for being har today," she continued. This was our staff meeting, which we called dress rehearsal. For a fleeting second, I felt incredibly fine. Wait: *not* fine. "I know, despite the shar joy we bring to others on this great day, that it is a personal sacrifice to be here. For that, Mr. Wigley..." She gestured toward Wigley, who bowed so low his forehead nearly touched the floor. "and myself..." She lifted her hoop skirt and curtsied. "...offer our eternal gratitude."

The makeup exuded a strong scent, which made me nauseous. Maybe I should vomit; in the long run that was probably a winning strategy. No. I would tough it out. No puking, no drinking, I'd simply Take It Like A Man.

"Today is a very special day because I have invited, and he has accepted, a great friend to join us."

About these breasts: they were a mammoth, sheeny affair, hoisted like giant dirigibles at right angles to her chest. The cleavage alone deserved its own zip code. As I stood there, trying not to vomit, I focused on that cleavage, like a sailor seeking the horizon. The naked part of Mrs. Wigley's breasts were, like her face, positively covered in gook. An oily silver substance melded with a caky orangish substance, with the effect of a gas spill in the desert or a piece of modern art you didn't quite get.

"This guest is a highly respected man in the entertainment industry. Resides half the year in Hollywood, where his Connections are well documented." Every year, Mrs. W made some such dramatic announcement. There was always an anonymous well-connected Hollywood player, which meant there was always a chance we'd be discovered. "He is a man always on the prowl for new talent, and I assured him there was NO better breeding ground of talent than right here." The Well Connected Hollywood Guest motivated me beyond belief that first year, even the second, a little less the third. He was a little like Santa Claus: you kept trying to believe in him well after you were pretty sure he didn't exist. "He travels incognito, evaluating talent and, ahem, carrying recommendations back to his Studio. Be your best today, gentlemen and ladies."

Back in the kitchen, with the first booking due any minute, the Mexican kitchen help—wearing, by the way, white powdered wigs—prepped. Randall Montgomery, one of the Three Spirits, rinsed off a huge crystal punch bowl and placed it inside an obscure baseboard cabinet, along with a silver ladle. There was a staff Christmas tradition at The Old Curiosity Shop of building a large Suicide Punch, consisting of all unfinished drinks bused throughout the day. (Glasses with cigarette butts or other waste materials excepted.) We secretly built and built the Suicide Punch throughout the lunchtime slam—half a gin and tonic here, a few wasted gulps of Chardonnay there, sprinkle of vodka martini, a dash of ale, and so forth—then started secretly drinking the Suicide Punch around 2 o'clock. We kept drinking it through the post-dinner Scrooge Ball. Not me, not this year. My whole motivation was that tomorrow would be a new day. I did not want to get on that merry-go-round where the liquor you drank to cure yesterday's hangover became tomorrow's hangover, ad infinitum.

On the other hand, I was feeling pretty okay. Wait: *not* pretty okay.

In agonizingly clear detail, the day trudged on: tedious prep work I'd done over and over, in nearly the exact same manner, a thousand or more times; the wait staff's transformation from Townies and Aspiring Actors and College Kids into Victorian Misers, and British Lads, and 19th-century London Shopkeepers; the giddy arrival of guests; the hammed-up responses to requests for more water or salt. For reasons I couldn't explain, this hangover seemed to encapsulate, even to embrace, the seven or eight worst hangovers I'd ever experienced, like an all-star tribute to hangovers. Hangover after hangover seemed to take the mic to add a wretched thought, to recall a particular brand of unpleasantness, to burp or fart or just swoon. From time to time, I would be suddenly beset by the miraculous feeling that my Hall of Fame hangover was gone, all gone. Seconds later, I would realize: *not* all gone.

When I looked up, bubbly families energized the gas-lit Cratchit Courtyard, lovey dovey couples packed Pip Hall, and bachelors lined the Pickwick Public House bar. Tipsy and spirited patrons lined up— *queued*, sorry—outside the first floor co-ed bathroom, affectionately known as Our Mutual Friend. A couple carrying baggage checked into Master Humphrey's Suite. The band did their sound check in the Great Expectations Ballroom. For a flash, I thought my mood had swung, that I'd gotten a poof of that fairy angel dust that magically transforms the holiday ambiance into something unforgettable. Wait: no fairy angel dust.

Scooter MacKenzie, who played A Local Philanthropist, appeared through the door, carrying clay water jugs. "A merry Christmas, Mr. Scrooge, God save you!"

I let him have it, "You mean to call yourself a waiter? I take my oath, I've never seen water so determined to escape its prison." I poured water over his stunned head.

This got a big laugh from the customers, if not from Scooter MacKenzie. They enjoyed the pretense, even the showmanship. But at a certain point, they wanted you to be a waiter. Grinding fresh pepper on the salad was a lot more critical than nailing a Cockney accent. Just wait. I had more for them. I took inspiration from this wretched hangover of mine to really slip into the role of Scrooge. I *was* him: God, did I despise people, God was I selfish, God how I wanted just to be left alone. I made sharp retorts on subjects ranging from bad teeth to fat—*portly*, my mistake—asses. I verbally punished customers and co-workers and especially the Wigleys. I deliberately brought out cold food, refused to substitute sides or leave anchovies off the Caesar's salad.

Some customers, whom I despised, were enchanted with my performance, while other customers, whom I also despised, were highly annoyed. The same trick occurred to them all, namely to wish me, "Merry Christmas!!!" in bright, cheerful, giggling holiday voices. "Merry?" I spit back. "What right have you to be merry? You've so little hair it won't, absolutely won't, be swooped the great bald distance of that shiny dome. And that nose? How singular!!! It brings to mind Punch and Judy, and on my soul I believe you're more inclined toward Judy."

I'd started out, way back, as an aspiring improv comedian, even went to Second City in Toronto for training. That comedic instinct partnered with my hangover-induced disgust of humanity to form a perfectly blended spite. I scattered *Bah! Humbugs!* liberally and with great feeling. An old bag in cheap costume jewelry signaled me over to her table. By now, Wigley and Mrs. W appeared somewhat nervous. Nervous enough, I thought, to fire me—no, *give me the sack*. Mrs. W. floated, between tinkles of the Please Ring For Assistance bell, from the Little Dorrit Guest Lodge to my station in the Cratchit Courtyard, to monitor the worrisome proceedings. Mrs. W's breasts preceded Mrs. W. herself by a good ten seconds coming and going, like a dirigible escort. Wigley, as host, turned his bulbous nose from his podium near the entrance to cast me a disapproving glance, though he appeared to be casting the family cat Nickleby a disapproving glance. The old bag began, "Hello, Mr. Scrooge." Her wrinkled face asked encouragement from her fellow diners, who snickered their approval. The old bag's husband lifted his disposable camera for a snapshot. "I want par-TIK-u-larrr-ly to wish you a Merry Christmas on this bless-ed day." She seemed highly satisfied with her goading, but I thwarted her smugness.

"I want par-TIK-u-larrrrrrrrrrrrrrrrrrrrrrrrrrrr-ly to avert my eyes from such an awful excuse for jewelry," I shot back. I'd hit a sore spot; I was hitting all sore spots. "My God, dear woman, is there no Charity Shop safe from your callow, unsophisticated taste? I swear, I would not hope such a necklace on the humblest peasant at the soup kitchen. Merry, indeed. Do you wish to suggest you're merry over cheap baubles and a most singular blend of perfume that would make a brothel blush? I say to your imitation pearls: Cheerio in hell!!!"

Things went on this way. I noticed Mrs. W in conference with Wigley, which was like the puppet master pulling the strings. Soon after, he approached. "Can we have a private conversation?" he asked, in a low voice, while seeming to study a tipsy grandma slurping her potato soup.

"Nay," I shouted. "I take my oath, Fred, you can take this holiday and leave me to my own accounts." Wigley grabbed my collar. He pressed his face near mine, and stared directly into my eyes, though he appeared to stare directly at the angel atop the Christmas tree. "The Hollywood Connection, sir…" he began.

"Humbug!" I denounced, and tore away.

It was exhausting. I'd gotten through nearly the whole lunch and early dinner fiasco. I took a break in the kitchen. All my younger actor colleagues, still convinced they were different than all us others *exactly* like themselves, darted into and out of the kitchen. Trays and plates were picked up and carried away. Salads were tossed. Champagne popped. Amidst this clamor, the Three Spirits, and The Coach and Six Driver, and Bob Cratchit, and Caroline Cratchit, and The Butcher, etc. squatted down, dipped the ladle into the Suicide Punch bowl, took big swigs, and continued on their now merry ways. I vaguely heard all their compliments and congratulations as I rubbed my temples. I hated my job. I hated the Wigleys. I hated myself. I would gladly have traded all my unborn children for the chance to lie down on my couch.

Then Perry Cromwell, aka Jacob Marley's Ghost, floated into the changing room. He wore a greatcoat over pantaloons and scraggly black

boots. He'd gotten the part because of his long, flowing hair, which was done in a pigtail. A chain was fastened around his stomach, wound down his legs and trailed behind him. It was made of cash-boxes, keys, padlocks, ledgers, deeds and heavy purses wrought in steel. He had a folded kerchief about his head and chin.

"Dude," he said to me. "I think there's really a Hollywood Agent out there. Mrs. W was out there all kissing his ass and sending complimentary champagne."

"It doesn't signify," I said. "The logic by which a gentleman producer would travel to our humble village is all asunder."

"Whatever, dude. Wigley tells me it's time for the transformation." The transformation coincided with dusk, when the Wigleys threw the switch on the courtyard Christmas tree. Customers viewed the show from the main dining room. "He said to say this is the moment that defines Scrooge. Said you'd know what that meant, and he was counting on you."

I felt like I could not go on another second, yet I knew it was only decent of me to finish out the day. As hard as it was, I would just have to tell the Wigleys, definitively, this was my Curtain Call. Marley's Ghost hoisted the ladle to my mouth, his hand cupped below to catch any spills. "Here," he said. "You need this."

The smell of fruit mingled with beer and gin. There was more than a little eggnog in there. I inhaled. The predominant smell, the evil that outdid the other evils for attention, was tequila—the very dog that had bitten me. The aroma cleared my sinuses. My head felt, briefly, lighter. I stared down into the milky punch, followed a lime sliver as it floated about the contaminated surface. An escape route to this dark alleyway presented itself. I sipped. I drank the whole ladle, then grabbed it from Perry. I went to the Suicide Punch Bowl. I wanted just a little more, I had to have more, I was mad for more. A lot more. I drank one after another ladle full. I felt suddenly miraculously all better. Wait: *yes*, suddenly miraculously all better. I smiled. When I raised my head, all my wonderfully talented colleagues smiled back. I noticed, for the first time, the beautiful shiny ornaments strung around the kitchen's borders. Everything was so fuzzy and warm.

"Merry Christmas," I giggled, to my already-smashed colleagues.

"You need to be thinking about lag time, yeah," Jacob Marley's ghost advised. "This stuff isn't like ordinary stuff; it'll hit you ka-Bam, and keep on hitting you." I could feel it, like a prescription starting to work. I drank more. More. The room seemed bright and fast and soft. It was hard to believe I hadn't moved from the punch bowl in twenty minutes. I loved my job. I loved the Wigleys. I loved myself.

I went over to Mary Ellen, aka Caroline Cratchit, whom I'd always had a little crush on, and said, "Dear Ms. Cratchit, it would be ungentle-manly of me not to wish you the most sincere and profound good cheer." I accepted her hand. She fake batted her eyelashes. I lightly brushed my lips to her skin, then jerked her into me and laid a nice, wet kiss on her mouth. "Merry Christmas, dear Ms. Cratchit," I whispered.

My colleagues burst out in applause. "Well done, that," Mary Ellen whispered back.

Jacob Marley's ghost grabbed my hand. "Great, man. You're there." He led me to the swinging double doors, then literally pushed me out into the courtyard. I stumbled. I ran forward, my arms fluttering at my side to keep balance. I screamed, "Hallo, whoop, hallo, whoop, whoop, whoop."

The dining room din paused. Heads turned my way. Mrs. W hustled toward us, as if responding to an emergency. Wigley's head craned in my direction, though his eyes seemed to follow a small boy's ramble to the bathroom—*loo*, excuse me. The old bag lady lifted her head. Other customers I'd terrorized acknowledged my whooping.

The courtyard Christmas tree flickered, flickered, and then a festive outline burst forth, as if from nothing, against the grainy dusk. Gasps and awws filled the room.

"Merry Christmas!!!" I yelled. "Merry Christmas!!!" I dipped my hand into my tip pocket. I pulled out the crumpled bills and sticky coins, threw them up in the air. Money floated, crashed, bounced around me. "The next round," I yelled, "is on me." The customers broke out in spon-taneous applause. I grabbed a champagne glass from a passing tray. I hopped onto a nearby vacant chair. I tinked the glass. "Grab your spirits one and all," I requested.

My co-workers were right there to back me. God, what great co-workers I had!!! They scrambled around their stations, filling glasses with the house red, offering alternative beverages, topping off glasses. "Hallo," I started, and then rambled through a five-minute toast that included the words "glorious" and "wonderful" no fewer than a dozen times each.

I jumped down from the chair. I ran from table to table, shaking hands and offering holiday cheer. I loved all my customers. What great customers! I really had the best customers anywhere.

As I surveyed the bright, cheerful landscape, filled with wonderful people on a wonderful holiday as dusk settled wonderfully beyond, I noted the customer with the free champagne. He looked, from my somewhat blurred vantage point, as if, indeed, he might be the Incognito Hollywood Agent; he certainly had an Incognito Hollywood Agent air about him. I even heard, unless I was mistaken, a distinct, "Bravo" come from his direction. That old fantasy flashed through my mind, and I let it. Why not? Today was a day not so much of miracles, but of belief in miracles.

The Courthouse lights dimmed, and a floodlight fell on the entrance. In hobbled Warren Wigley. Having traded his lamplighter outfit for crutches, the prepubescent, bulbous-nosed heir of Old Curiosity dragged his chunky, clunky body dramatically across the floor. He rolled his eyes in a manner that suggested gassy more than cancer-stricken. His lips moved silently, over and over the same words. "God Bless us, everyone," he blurted, as if relieving himself of a weight about to become too heavy.

What an absolutely priceless child!!! I ran up to the glorious child and patted him on the head. "God bless *you*," I told him. I looked up, glanced around the spinning, pirouetting, somersaulting, flip-flopping room. Wonderful decorations! Wonderful food!! Wonderful people!!! "God bless you," I declared, in my most humble voice.

Then, suspecting Suicide Punch might not be the impetus for real, genuine transformation but not wanting to rule it out, I yelled in my loudest, most emphatic voice yet, "GOD BLESS YOU, ONE AND ALL."

Ours Now

"Do-Good!!!" "Do-Good!!!"

Our cat was dead; there were no other real good explanations. Probably she'd become a petrified fur ball on some dirty roadside. Maybe she was a soft lump in a basement stairwell. "She might have found a nice cat friend," I offered.

My husband turned to call one way down the block. "Do-Good!!!" "Do-Good!!!" I called the other. We rotated. "Do-Good!!!" "Do-Good!!!" Benjamin and I peered between houses, under bushes, to the tops of trees. Ever since that first winter on the farm, DoGood had always returned inside a few hours. Now, it had been five long days.

"Do-Good!!!!!!" My husband's face crackled with sadness. DoGood might have been flattened by a reckless street sweeper. Smooshed by a mean dump truck. Crushed beneath a horrible, cheery-colored SUV.

"I'll bet," I said, "some little girl started feeding her treats."

We paused. It was the week before Christmas. Our front yard seemed like this incredibly tiny space, and everything beyond it big and terrifying. Our lungs filled with air. We prepared to once again scream our cat's name.

Through the steamed glass of my greenhouse, I watched the neighbor lady gingerly approach. She rapped on the door. "It's open," I said.

A cold breeze traveled along the dirt near my ankles. "Hi, Janey," she said, lifting her burlap dress with two fingers as she settled herself on a bench near the goldfish fountain. "My, how you're able to make things grow."

We'd lived in our new house more than a year. Until DoGood went missing, the neighbor woman hadn't so much as introduced herself. Now, she made daily stops.

"Well, the chemo treatments start tomorrow," she said. "I'm scared but upbeat."

Lily had some relatively mild strain of cancer—which kind I can't remember, one of the bad kinds. That first day, after I'd given her the garden tour—*here are the azaleas, and the American roses, there are the orchids, the maypops*—she opened up. A juvenile delinquent teenaged son. An abusive ex-husband. A leaky roof. The cancer. Lily was 42 years old, just six years older than my husband, five years older than me. I reflected on the fact that people our age had grown children and deadly diseases. We weren't young anymore.

"Stay strong, Lily, that's all you can do." I didn't know what to say. I felt bad, but Lily's undisguised anguish somehow canceled out my sympathy. They'd given her a 70 percent chance of full recovery, which seemed pretty good until you thought about the 30 percent. Still, I would rather she'd suffered in silence.

"I'm doing just that. Say, that cat of yours, it had white paws?"

All our adult lives, my husband and I had individually struggled with debt and career issues. We'd both knocked down the kind of doctorate degrees that lead to hard-to-get, shitty-paying jobs. We climbed and climbed those ladders. Then we met, got married, and combined our huge debts and huge career problems. We'd always thought we'd have time to decide: do we have kids or not? Benjamin, at various times, had finally concluded, *Yes*, but I'd voted for postponement. Then I'd finally concluded, *Yes*, but Ben had wanted postponement. It was always, "Once he makes managing editor," "After I'm tenured," "As soon as we get the second mortgage paid down." It had gotten to where we had to do it if we were going to do it. DoGood had been a meek compromise, though neither of us put it like that.

Lily scattered DoGood inquiries between cancer updates and juvie court results. Had we called the shelter? Did we try down by the creek? Any calls off the flyers?

"Yes, white paws and a white beard and a white belly, black otherwise," I said.

"Its name, again?"

"DoGood," I said. "It was the alias Benjamin Franklin used when he started writing letters for his brother's newspaper at the age of 16."

"That's right," Lily remembered. "Ben is related." Benjamin Franklin DuPont, my husband, descended from the storied 18th century statesman. You would think Ben's ancestry had little to do with anything, but it came up almost instantly the first time he met somebody. Early on, I'd been a little impressed with the fact myself.

"How old is DoGood?"

"Around six, maybe seven," I said. "We're not sure; she was a feral cat when we got her." We had adopted DoGood five years before. We were living on a remote farmhouse in the Amanas, with no social network whatsoever. It was lovely there in the country, especially in the spring and autumn. We became sensitized to the subtle shades of white in winter and green in summer. We enjoyed one after another glorious sunset sky. Sometimes, we just sipped wine and listened to the crickets in the pitch-black night, or watched the firefly-lit field glow. But like I said: no people.

We fed the birds, we fed the rabbits, we fed the cats. Deer, raccoons, possums. We even fed a skunk. We gave all the cats elaborate names out of medical journals, gardening books, newspaper lore or Franklin family history. Petunia. Royko. Lightning. Scarlet.

DoGood was the one who stayed. We courted her for months and months. Every morning, we found her perched atop the storage crate next to our back door. She'd peer into the kitchen. She'd run away when we opened the door to set out the food bowl, sneak back when we were gone. We laughed and cooed at her from the kitchen. She made low guttural noises as she gobbled the food, like a lion with a kill. She was an undersized female with twinkling whiskers, a pink button nose, and intelligent gray eyes. Feral but cute. Very cute.

She greeted our first attempts to touch her with hisses. Gradually, she let us get closer. Closer. Closer. That first time DoGood raised her head to be petted, it was like smacking the Prom King right on the lips. It had taken such exhaustive and creative measures to seduce DoGood into liking us, trusting us, that it seemed like a tiny miracle.

"These cats adjust just fine," Lily said. "Believe me, they're smart about it: they find good homes for themselves."

I'd heard owls swooped down on cats, that snakes swallowed them whole. I could only imagine the terror of DoGood's final, awful moments.

"Sure," I said. "There's a reason people say cats always land on their feet."

"Do-Good! Do-Good!" It had become habitual: each time we left the house. "Do-Good! Do-Good!!" After a time, I hardly noticed we were doing it. On our way to the car—"Do-Good!!"—as we prepared for our daily walk around the neighborhood—DO-GOOD—when we set out the garbage—DO-GOOD. When we went down the block for the newspaper—DO-GOOD, DO-GOOD, DO-GOOD.

"We should have never tried moving a country cat to the city," Ben said.

We fastened ourselves into our Ford Explorer. Ben had a theory, based on something a colleague read or might have heard, that DoGood, lost, would try to find her way the 20 miles back to our old farmhouse. I drove. The splendor of winter was all about us. Snow covered the harvested fields like a blanket over a napping baby. Brittle corn husks floated listlessly above icy gravel roads. We crawled along wide-open fields, past crumbling barns and silos, around pigpens. Hawks eyed us from fence post perches. This drive made me nostalgic, but I had no desire to return to that life. I had an urge to be sweet, to tell Ben that I liked then and I liked now, and if this was the trajectory of our lives then we were very lucky. But I didn't. Since DoGood went missing, probably before that, there'd been a vague, unacknowledged tension between us, and I was wishing for that to pass on its own.

We cautiously turned into our old driveway. The steep incline led us around the side of the house to the back. The porch swing we'd left swayed with a breeze. We used to sit there at harvest time, DoGood's favorite time of year. As rows of corn came down, hundreds of field mice scurried for new homes. DoGood would lay fully stretched on her belly, her eyes trained on the next victim. She'd spring. It would be hard on anybody who sympathized with the mice, but it was a regular carnival for us cat fans.

We knocked. A scraggly dad in denim overalls, two boys and a girl hanging around his knees, opened the back door. Without asking who we were, he indicated for us to come inside. We stayed in the warm entryway. "We're here about a cat," we said, and went on to explain everything.

"Lots a cats here," the dad said. "Too many. They's people drive out here just to dump an unwanted litter." We described DoGood, but the dad shrugged, indicating one cat was the same as another. I bet he could pick a cow out of a lineup, though. He stooped to his kids, "Any of you seen this lady's cat?"

The children ticked off everything they knew about every cat they'd seen, which was a lot. "Can we just look around a bit?" I asked. The dad indicated it was okay. He added, "Take any of 'em that'll let you; we aren't attached."

We searched the garage, the hog shed that no longer housed hogs, the woodworking shed; all the potential hiding spots. The cold was getting to be too much. "The woman at the shelter said cats do get disoriented," Ben said. "Lots of times it takes a while but they find their ways."

DoGood was some fox's lunch. She was a garbage truck's hood ornament. A poster kitty for some deadly cat disease.

"Absolutely," I said. "She's got to somehow get her bearings."

Lily's scarf appeared as a bright red smudge against the greenhouse glass. Lily caned her way up our ornamental stone path to the door. She banged once with the cane while simultaneously creaking open the door. I scooped dirt from a wheelbarrow into a clay pot. She looked frailer than last I'd seen her, and she was frail then. I jammed the spade into the dirt. I'd extracted this dirt from outside, where the hard earth fought my spade. It had defrosted some, but still showed a blacker face than dusty summer soil.

Lily always arrived from the south. She'd said which was her house and I think I knew the one she meant, but I'd never actually seen her in that context. Once inside, Lily's eyes darted everywhere but towards me; then she sort of sighed.

"Well, I went ahead and changed all the locks."

She handed me a department store bag, the paper kind with handles. I looked inside: a tea cozy adorned with floral prints.

"I saw that you drink your tea in here. This is a little something to keep the pot warm," she said. "The boy, when he's not off smoking pot or spray painting walls, he helps me with my knitting projects these days. Goes gets the supplies, at least."

Lily had taken to bringing me little gifts each time she visited. Wall hangings, seeds, a pie once, ear muffs. "Thanks, this will come in handy."

Lily looked out over the greenhouse, as if she were doing inventory. "Well, they say the first treatment is always a shock, so I shouldn't be surprised it beat me up like it did."

"I like the red scarf." I didn't know why Lily had chosen me as her confidante. I couldn't imagine I'd said anything vaguely reassuring or wise. I found, though I couldn't admit it, that Lily annoyed me slightly. I was four years into a lifetime of research into the dengue virus. I mostly enjoyed my work, and knew I was doing my little bit to make the world better, but there were lots of headaches: funding issues, political in-fighting, needy and annoying student aides, all the big To Do lists. My confidence and determination, not to mention my stamina and faith, sometimes wavered. The greenhouse was where I retreated to mull things over, reenergize, or just relax. But here was Lily, making me sorry for her. She reminded me of my mortality and advancing age, stirred the Kids-No Kids pot, issued cautionary tales about how far wrong everything could go, none of which fell into the category of Taking A Load Off.

"Oh, yes, thank you. There's been no hair loss yet; this is more of a preemptive strike. That way, when I do lose the hair it'll seem only natural that I'm wearing head pieces."

It struck me as odd, how Lily opened up like she did. I would never in a million years have considered telling her, say, about my thyroid problem. Or problems between Ben and me. But I figured that was the way some people were. On paper Lily was one of those sweet, down-on-her-luck women you weren't allowed to dislike. What would it sound like to find fault? *My cancer-stricken neighbor stops by once in a while to give me gifts and chat about my garden, to console me about my lost pet, to show an interest in my work. God, do I hate her.*

"It looks good," I said.

Lily stared at my Christmas roses. I stared with her, spade in my hand. I didn't know whether I was to keep working as we chatted, or to stop working so we could chat.

Then, "I saw your signs." In my head, I had considered them posters or flyers and so at first *signs* didn't register. "What kind of kitty was your little kitty again?" I didn't like how she used the past tense.

"We think it's a Domestic Shorthair, but probably, almost surely, a mixed breed."

"Yes, okay," she said. "It's on the sign that way, isn't it?"

We had just put up a new round. The headline said, "Lost Cat," with details such as breed, size, and temperament. I'd gotten so choked up picking out the pictures: DoGood in endless, loving, adorable poses. I recognized that our lives were now irretrievably different than before and that all attempts at continuity a sham, but I didn't know what to do with that insight. Ben had said the first flyers had by now been taken down or blown off their telephone posts. We needed to keep up our end. "DoGood could be roaming the neighborhood," Ben had said.

DoGood was roaming kitty heaven. I had told Ben, "Sure, she could be right around the corner, just confused." We had split up and covered a three-mile radius.

Lying in bed later, Ben had said, "I think if we don't find her by Christmas..." I'd looked over at Ben's deflated, slumped body. He, no more than I, thought we'd actually find DoGood. Even on the improbable chance DoGood was alive, she would never allow herself to be captured and returned. After years of lying in our laps, sleeping on my neck at night, purring as she nestled between Ben and me, DoGood still would not go near other people.

Lily sat cross-legged on the bench, deep in thought. She looked as though she had just regrettably concluded there was no answer to her riddle. She sighed again.

I'd thought before about how it would be for Ben and me to grow old together with kids, and how it would be for Ben and me to grow old together without kids. Looking at Lily's bright red scarf, I started to think how it would be for one of us to grow old without the other. Without anybody.

Ben jiggled the key into our door as I balanced groceries in either hand. The phone rang inside the apartment. Ben rushed to catch it. As I set the groceries on the kitchen table, Ben frantically indicated for me to get a pen and paper, then signaled that I should get on the other line.

"I didn't get a long look at her," the man's voice said. "But from what I saw it looked like the cat on the poster."

"Where is she now?" Ben asked.

"Last I saw, she darted under the neighbor's porch. You might have trouble finding her again, but that's where she was. Come take a look around."

I sweated through my winter coat. Hope pierced my center like a lightning bolt. I mentally prepared for how I would handle this if it were a false alarm, what I would say to Ben.

"Where are you at?" Ben said.

"Over on South Mariposa Street," the man said.

We were on South Mariposa Street. There could be no doubting now, DoGood was alive. "Across from the Health Center," the man said.

As we raced out the door, we told each other not to be overly optimistic, that in all likelihood it was some other cat, some other black and white cat, but before we ever got to the car we both were sure: DoGood was out there. The man lived at the end of the block. We yelled DO-GOOD all the way from our door to his. He stood outside shivering against the winter chill, looking east then west. We approached him almost at a dead run. He said, "She was just here. Now she's gone."

We called, DO-GOOD. We called again. We walked around back of the man's house and yelled, through his gangway and yelled. My head was down as I checked under porches and cracked-open garage doors. When I looked up, there was the house I thought was probably Lily's house. I debated whether or not to enlist her help—she might have seen something, then again she might have just returned from a treatment. It might not even be her house.

As I circled the neighborhood, I wondered about my theory. I'd always thought of DoGood as ultimately loyal, I'd thought of her as content, but if she wasn't dead and was in fact steps away from our house.... was it possible she didn't want to come home? There was so little you could know for sure about a cat. I walked around and around, head down. As I lapped Lily's house again, I thought about the potential for showing up at a bad time, but then thought of all Lily's inquiries about DoGood, all the questions and sincere expressions of sympathy. I walked up her sidewalk and gently knocked on the door. The shades were drawn. The house appeared dark. My plan was, if she answered the light knock she was probably up for visitors. If not, not.

There was no answer.

After a bit, I spotted Ben turning in a slow circle beneath a dim streetlight. We both sat on the curb. Every few minutes, one or the other of us, sometimes both, weakly cried out, Do-Good.

We got two more calls after that first call. Both sightings were in that same general vicinity: down the block near Lily's house. It seemed sure

there was some black-and-white cat, if not DoGood then DoGood's look-alike. But now, Christmas Day had come and nearly gone, and as I studied Ben dozing in his chair I sheepishly snuck out the back door. I didn't yell. I was as little aware of not yelling Do-Good as I'd been of yelling DO-GOOD. We hoped for another sighting, but secretly thought we'd missed our best chance.

I guiltily looked back at the house. Christmas in a childless house lacks exuberance, and today we'd sorely missed our tradition of watching DoGood playfully paw at wrapped squeaky toys and bow-tied balls. It was just another day. We'd been having a running argument about all the time I spent in the greenhouse; Ben had noted that I chose to spend *our* precious time with flowers. "What does that say?" he'd demanded. I hadn't considered the psychological underpinnings, but after Ben's accusation I did notice I got restless when I tried to show restraint. I thought of that greenhouse like some people did their email or a secret lover.

It was already turning dark, and the cold was dramatic. I stepped into the greenhouse and luxuriated in the toasty, humid environment. I spread compost manure and peat around our Christmas Roses. I dug and divided some of the crowded clumps. I thought about the emotional turmoil of moving DoGood from the farm to our new place. Ben had gotten a good job offer on the city news desk, and I'd had about enough of the long commute into my lab. We'd read up on whether it was tougher for the cat to adjust to new surroundings or new people. But the literature, as it were, was decisively split. DoGood was whiny and needy and confused those first days in the new city apartment. She even refused to go outside. My outside garden, where DoGood had found refuge under big wisteria vines and drooping sunflowers, and the greenhouse became her comfort zones. Maybe this was all our fault.

I spotted Lily, a purple blur outside the glass. She wore a purple babushka and purple shawl, she was all purple. She used a silver walker now for support. I could not believe this frail woman was a mere five years older than me, that from where I was standing I was in striking distance of that.

"With that thaw we had the other day, I'm all out of buckets to catch the water coming through my roof. I don't know what I can do until the deadbeat catches up on some of his child support payments."

I set down my rake. I removed my right glove to scratch an itch. The wrinkled skin of Lily's forehead disappeared into the purple babushka the way a mountain peak meets the sky.

"Did you ever stop to think that I'm a Lily—in other words I'm named the same as a flower—and I'm here in your flower garden?"

"Lily in the garden," I said.

She took a deep breath. I could tell she had something traumatic to say. I'd feared this moment: I didn't know what to say or do if the treatments didn't go well and she got worse. What if the prognosis was death? I was ill equipped to console this woman, and resented, slightly, that I'd inherited the job.

Lily loosened the knot on her babushka. She removed the purple headpiece to reveal a smooth, completely bald head. She wiped her brow, placed the babushka back on top, tightened the knot. I was just about to wish Lily a Merry Christmas, when she said, almost in a whisper, "DoGood is my cat now." She stood fully erect and looked me in the eyes. Almost as soon as the words were out of Lily's mouth, a revised version of my life passed before my eyes. I thought about all those two-hour periods between when DoGood darted out our back door and returned. I thought of Lily spying on DoGood out her back window as we'd spied on DoGood out our farmhouse window. I thought of Lily setting out food as we'd set out food, of DoGood rubbing against Lily's legs as she'd rubbed against our legs. I thought of the time when DoGood finally mustered the courage to enter Lily's house, as she'd entered our farmhouse. I pictured DoGood exploring the basement, the closets, all around, ever with an eye toward the door. I thought about that threshold DoGood must have crossed when, finally, she preferred to stay rather than leave.

"What do you mean, Lily?" I knew what she meant. I didn't know whether to be happy because DoGood was alive, angry because Lily had stolen her, or sad because the loss was so personal. I struggled in that brief moment with a rush of monumental betrayal—not by Lily, but by DoGood.

"I had no idea in the beginning that this precious little cat belonged to anybody. She had no tags, you know. She had been coming to my house a long time before the flyers told me some more of the story. I learned the rest from you here, but by then.... Janey, you know this cancer has been so tough on me, plus all my other troubles..." She stopped silent. Lily was not pleading; she was explaining. She had no intention of giving DoGood back.

"She's ours now," she stated.

What were my options? I suppose I could have demanded DoGood back, though Lily might have battled that like she did her cancer. We could have immediately begun counter-seduction techniques, courted DoGood with fresh fish and tartar-flavored treats. But standing there in my garden I found myself feeling the way Lily felt, that this conversation brought closure to the affair.

"Well, believe you me, we got tags for Lazi. That's her name now, after Peregrine Laziosi, the Patron Saint of Cancer Patients."

It came down to that, in Lily's mind: she'd bought identification tags and we hadn't. Lily turned and left. I stared at the greenhouse door, watching this purple lump battle her way south, against the wind and cold and everything else that had teamed up on her. I looked into the sky and was surprised to see the moon. Days were so short now. I strained to make out the pattern of stars just showing themselves against the darkening sky. All those little dots, each with slightly different voltage, some bright, some dim. I thought about the old wives tale regarding the nine lives of cats. How many lives were there before DoGood? How many remained after Lazi?

I opened the back door and smelled vanilla pudding. Bill Monroe's live version of *Cotton-Eyed Joe* played on the boom box, and Ben stirred and danced at the same time. I stood in a shaft of moonlight at the doorway, watching my handsome, happy husband. He brushed a bang back from his forehead. I was relieved that he seemed okay with my greenhouse visit, but anxious over how to break the DoGood news. I snuck up behind him, kissed him gently on the neck, then the ear. He laughed. "Puddings's almost ready, honey," he said.

"Forget about pudding," I said.

I lowered the flame, led Ben by the hand to the bedroom. I watched him undress. As we lay warm and naked under the blanket, I whispered, "Let's start trying."

I thought about how much joy DoGood had given us, and on the other hand what heartbreak came of it all. I thought about overpopulation, and the selfishness of having a child we weren't positive we wanted. But none of that mattered at the moment. We would begin trying. With luck, there would be a young Ben Franklin before another Christmas passed. If not, we'd try fertility drugs. Or adopt. Maybe we'd adopt a Mexican baby Ben, or a Chinese baby Benny. Perhaps there would be an Iranian brother or sister down the road. It didn't matter: I wanted to fill the house with love in all sizes and colors.

I brushed my hand against Ben's skin. My whole body trembled, or perhaps tingled—the two sensations shared so many of the same qualities, it was hard to tell them apart.

Donald G. Evans is the author of the novel *Good Money After Bad* and editor of *Cubbie Blues: 100 Years of Waiting Till Next Year;* his short stories have been published in a variety of literary journals. He is the founding executive editor of the Chicago Literary Hall of Fame, has been listed four times in the Newcity *Lit 50: Who Really Books in Chicago* feature, and received the Chicago Writers Association's Spirit Award for lifetime achievement. He won a residency at Saltonstall Arts Colony and was an artist-in-residence at Cliff Dwellers Club. He has taught at a variety of institutions, most recently as a lecturer at Newberry Library. He lives just outside Chicago with his wife Margaret and son Dusty. Find more at DonadGEvans.com.

Hannah Jennings has designed and illustrated countless books, websites, and signs that interpret exhibits in zoos and museums. The focus of her MFA from the School of the Art Institute of Chicago was her artist's books; she now teaches design at Dominican University. She is past president of the Society for Experiential Graphic Design. Her love of design, making images, and Christmas is apparent in her non-traditional online advent calendars; see them with her other illustrations at HannahJennings.com.